Life Science

REINFORCEMENT & VOCABULARY REVIEW WORKSHEETS

This book was printed with soy-based ink on acid-free recycled content paper, containing 10% POSTCONSUMER WASTE.

HOLT, RINEHART AND WINSTON

A Harcourt Classroom Education Company

Austin • New York • Orlando • Atlanta • San Francisco • Boston • Dallas • Toronto • London

To the Teacher

These worksheets are designed to help you reinforce the vocabulary and concepts students need to build a solid foundation in the sciences. Key concepts are reviewed in the Reinforcement Worksheets. Key terms are stressed in the Vocabulary Review Worksheets. This booklet contains one Vocabulary Review Worksheet and at least one Reinforcement Worksheet for each chapter in the *Holt Science and Technology* Pupil's Edition.

▪ Reinforcement Worksheets

By approaching a topic that is discussed in the Pupil's Edition from a different angle, such as with visual aids or within the framework of a new scenario, these worksheets help move students from frustration to understanding. You can use Reinforcement Worksheets in a variety of ways, such as to do the following:

- target the students in the class who are struggling to understand a concept
- gauge how well the class is understanding a topic before you formally assess the topic or before you move on to a new, progressive topic
- provide a refresher of a topic discussed in the last class period
- conclude a lesson by revisiting and reinforcing an essential topic
- instill confidence as students complete these enjoyable and doable worksheets
- provide opportunities for group work and cooperative learning

▪ Vocabulary Review Worksheets

With puzzles, crosswords, word searches, and other unintimidating challenges, the Vocabulary Review Worksheets can help your students do the following:

- remember important vocabulary terms for each chapter
- review and study vocabulary definitions
- think critically about the way in which the words are used in talking about science
- warm up for a new lesson by starting out with a puzzle
- participate in cooperative learning activities by solving puzzles with a partner or group

Answer Key

For your convenience, an Answer Key is provided in the back of this booklet. The key includes reduced versions of all applicable worksheets with answers included.

Art Credits

All art unless otherwise noted, by Holt, Rinehart and Winston. All work, unless otherwise noted, contributed by Holt, Rinehart and Winston. Abbreviated as follows: (t) top; (b) bottom; (l) left; (r) right; (c) center; (bkgd) background.
Front cover (owl), Kim Taylor/Bruce Coleman, Inc.; (forest), Carr Clifton; (jaquar), © Gerry Ellis/GerryEllis.com; Page 6 (c), Accurate Art, Inc.; 11 (t), Laurie O'Keefe; 12 (b), Carlyn Iverson; 16 (t), Carlyn Iverson; 38 (tl), Laurie O'Keefe; 38 (cl), Laurie O'Keefe; 38 (bl), Laurie O'Keefe; 38 (tr), Laurie O'Keefe; 38 (cr), Laurie O'Keefe; 38 (br), Laurie O'Keefe; 41 (t), Carlyn Iverson; 41 (b), Carlyn Iverson; 43 (tl), Carlyn Iverson; 43 (tr), Carlyn Iverson; 43 (bl), Carlyn Iverson; 43 (br), Carlyn Iverson; 54 (tl), Laurie O'Keefe; 54 (cl), Laurie O'Keefe; 54 (bl), Laurie O'Keefe; 64 (c), Layne Lundstrom; 67 (r), Laurie O'Keefe; 68 (b), Laurie O'Keefe; 72 (t), Laurie O'Keefe; 82 (c), Laurie O'Keefe.

Printed in the United States of America

ISBN 0-03-055659-7 5 6 085 03 02

CONTENTS

CONTENTS, CONTINUED

CONTENTS, CONTINUED

Name ______________________ Date ____________ Class ____________

CHAPTER

REINFORCEMENT WORKSHEET

The Mystery of the Bubbling Top

Complete this worksheet after you have finished reading Chapter 1, Section 2.

Use the materials at right to conduct the activity below. Then answer the questions that follow.

MATERIALS

- small, empty plastic soda bottle
- cold water
- plastic or plastic-foam disposable plate
- scissors
- hot water
- beaker or other container large enough to hold the soda bottle

1. Fill the empty bottle halfway with cold water.

2. Cut a quarter-sized disk from the plastic plate.

3. Moisten the plastic disk, and place it on top of the bottle's neck.

4. Pour hot water into the beaker until it is about one-quarter full.

5. Carefully place the bottle inside the beaker.

6. What happened to the plastic disk?

____

____

____

You just made observations.

7. Why do you think the plastic disk did that? Brainstorm for as many answers as possible. Then put a star next to the explanation you consider most reasonable.

____

____

____

____

____

You just formed a hypothesis.

8. How could you test your hypothesis? Outline an experiment you could conduct.

____

____

____

____

9. Conduct your experiment. What happens?

____

____

You just tested your hypothesis.

10. How do you explain the results of your experiment?

____

____

____

____

You just analyzed the results of your experiment.

11. Do the results of your experiment match your hypothesis? Explain.

____

____

____

____

12. Do you need to conduct more experiments to find out if your hypothesis is correct? Why or why not?

____

____

____

____

____

You just drew conclusions.

Congratulations!
You have just finished the first steps of the scientific method!
Share your results with your classmates.

Name ______________________________ Date ______________ Class ____________

CHAPTER 1 **VOCABULARY REVIEW WORKSHEET**

The Puzzling World of Life Science

Try this puzzle after you finish reading Chapter 1.
Using each of these clues, fill in the blanks provided on the next page with the letters of the word or phrase described below.

1. the use of knowledge, tools, and materials to solve problems and accomplish tasks
2. a unifying explanation for a broad range of hypotheses and observations that have been supported by testing
3. the measure of an object's surface
4. liquid that freezes at 0°C and boils at 100°C
5. the amount of space that something occupies
6. used for almost a century to see internal body structures
7. A ________ ________ tests one factor at a time.
8. made before scientists can test a hypothesis, stated as "if . . . , then . . ."
9. A ________ ________ microscope has a tube with lenses, a stage, and a light source.
10. the study of living things
11. Scientists draw ________ after organizing and analyzing the data from an experiment.
12. the one factor that differs in a controlled experiment
13. set of steps scientists use to answer a question or solve a problem
14. measured in kelvins or degrees Celsius
15. the amount of matter that makes up an object
16. anything in an experiment that can influence the outcome of the experiment
17. uses short bursts of a magnetic field to produce images (abbreviation)
18. possible answer to a question
19. uses electrons to produce magnified images
20. Scientists ________ their results to other scientists after they complete their investigations.
21. basic unit of length in SI

Name ______________________ Date ______________ Class ______________

1. T ___ ___ ___ ___ ___ ___ ___ ___ ___ ___

2. ___ H ___ ___ ___ ___

3. ___ ___ E ___

4. W ___ ___ ___ ___

5. ___ O ___ ___ ___ ___

6. ___ R ___ ___ ___

7. ___ ___ ___ ___ ___ ___ L ___ ___ ___   ___ ___ ___ ___ ___ ___ ___ ___ ___ ___

8. ___ ___ ___ D ___ ___ ___ ___ ___ ___

9. ___ O ___ ___ ___ ___ ___ ___   ___ ___ ___ ___ ___

10. ___ ___ F ___   ___ ___ ___ ___ ___ ___ ___

11. ___ ___ ___ ___ L ___ ___ ___ ___ ___ ___

12. ___ ___ ___ I ___ ___ ___ ___

13. ___ ___ ___ ___ ___ ___ ___ F ___ ___   ___ ___ ___ ___ ___ ___

14. ___ ___ ___ ___ E ___ ___ ___ ___ ___ ___

15. ___ ___ ___ S

16. ___ ___ C ___ ___ ___

17. ___ ___ I

18. ___ ___ ___ ___ ___ ___ E ___ ___ ___

19. ___ ___ ___ ___ ___ ___ ___ N   ___ ___ ___ ___ ___ ___ ___ ___ ___ ___

20. ___ ___ ___ ___ ___ ___ ___ C ___ ___ ___

21. ___ ___ ___ E ___

Name ______________________ Date ____________ Class ____________

CHAPTER 2 REINFORCEMENT WORKSHEET

Amazing Discovery

Complete this worksheet after you finish reading Chapter 2, Section 2.

Imagine that you are a biologist on a mission to Mars. You have just discovered what you think is a simple single-celled Martian organism. For now, you are calling it Alpha. Before you can claim that you have discovered life on Mars, however, you need to show that Alpha is alive.

1. What are the six characteristics you will look for to see if Alpha is alive?

a. ______________________

b. ______________________

c. ______________________

d. ______________________

e. ______________________

f. ______________________

2. Outline a test or experiment to verify one of the characteristics you listed above.

____

____

____

____

____

____

____

____

3. If you can show that Alpha is alive, you will take it back to Earth for further study. What will you need to provide Alpha with to keep it alive?

____

____

____

Name ______________________ Date ______________ Class ____________

CHAPTER 2

REINFORCEMENT WORKSHEET

Building Blocks

Complete this worksheet after you finish reading Chapter 2, Section 3.

Each of the boxes below represents one of the five compounds that are found in all cells. The phrases at the bottom of the page describe these compounds. Match each of the descriptions to the appropriate compound. Then write the corresponding letter in the appropriate box. Some descriptions may be used more than once.

Compounds in Cells

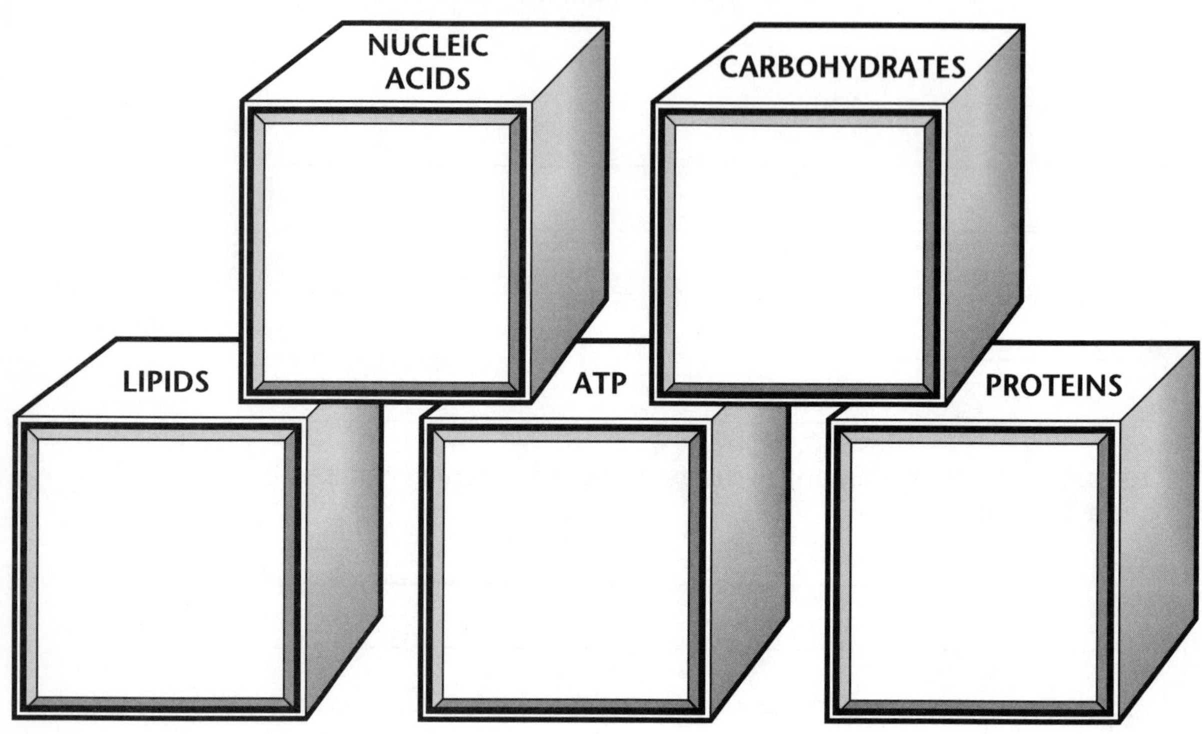

Clues

A. fat in animals

B. made of sugars

C. oil in plants

D. one type forms much of the cell membrane

E. enzymes

F. major fuel used for the cell's activities

G. "blueprints" of life

H. subunits are amino acids

I. hemoglobin

J. cannot mix with water

K. DNA

L. tells the cell how to make proteins

M. can be simple or complex

N. subunits called nucleotides

O. make up spider webs and hair

P. starch in plants

Q. source of stored energy

R. adenosine triphosphate

S. energy in lipids and carbohydrates is transferred to this molecule

Name ______________________ Date ______________ Class ______________

CHAPTER 2

VOCABULARY REVIEW WORKSHEET

It's Alive!

Complete this puzzle after you finish Chapter 2.

In the space provided, write the term described by the clue. Then find these words in the puzzle. Terms can be hidden in the puzzle vertically, horizontally, diagonally or backwards.

1. ______________ change in an organism's environment that affects the activity of an organism
2. ______________ group of compounds made of sugars
3. ______________ maintenance of a stable internal environment
4. ______________ complex carbohydrate made by plants
5. ______________ transmission of characteristics from one generation to the next
6. ______________ chemical activities of an organism necessary for life
7. ______________ made up of subunits called nucleotides
8. ______________ eats other organisms for food
9. ______________ organism that breaks down the nutrients of dead organisms or wastes for food
10. ______________ two layers of these form much of the cell membrane
11. ______________ proteins that speed up certain chemical reactions
12. ______________ molecule that provides instructions for making proteins
13. ______________ organism that can produce its own food
14. ______________ membrane-covered structure that contains all materials necessary for life
15. ______________ reproduction in which a single parent produces offspring that are identical to the parent
16. ______________ chemical compound that cannot mix with water and that is used to store energy
17. ______________ large molecule made up of amino acids
18. ______________ energy in food is transferred to this molecule
19. ______________ reproduction in which two parents are necessary to produce offspring that share characteristics of both parents

D	P	H	O	S	P	H	O	L	I	P	I	D	S
N	S	D	T	E	R	P	U	I	R	C	S	E	I
A	A	S	E	X	U	A	L	O	O	I	T	C	S
R	C	Y	Z	U	P	H	D	S	T	A	I	O	A
C	E	L	L	A	T	U	E	D	R	B	M	M	T
O	N	M	X	L	C	H	C	D	E	D	U	P	S
N	Z	E	H	E	C	E	Y	I	I	P	L	O	O
S	Y	O	R	R	I	H	A	P	L	L	U	S	E
U	M	N	A	R	O	L	I	U	X	C	S	E	M
M	E	T	A	B	O	L	I	S	M	Y	U	R	O
E	S	E	R	L	N	P	R	O	T	E	I	N	H
R	H	A	M	Z	Y	T	I	D	E	R	E	H	E
A	C	E	D	I	C	A	C	I	E	L	C	U	N

Name ______________________ Date ____________ Class ____________

CHAPTER

3 REINFORCEMENT WORKSHEET

Light Interactions

Complete this worksheet after you finish reading Chapter 3, Section 2.

Your good friend, Roy G. Biv, has written out a list of the ways light waves interact. Roy knows a lot about light waves, but he doesn't know the scientific terms. Help Roy arrange his notes so that every definition or example on his list is in the appropriate box below. Some notes may be used more than once.

Reflection	Absorption	Scattering

Roy's Notes on Light

- causes a flashlight beam to become dimmer the farther away from the flashlight it travels
- why a window glass feels warm on a sunny day
- why you detect green light coming from a lime
- why you do not detect red light coming from a lime
- occurs when light energy is released from particles that have extra energy
- allows you to see yourself in a mirror
- occurs when energy from light waves is transferred to particles in matter
- causes the sky to appear blue
- allows you to see objects outside the beam of light
- causes cats' eyes to glow at night
- affects light with short wavelengths more than light with long wavelengths
- occurs when a light wave bounces off an object

Name ____________________ Date ____________ Class ____________

CHAPTER 3 **VOCABULARY REVIEW WORKSHEET**

A Light Puzzle

Try this anagram after you finish Chapter 3.

Use the definitions below to unscramble the vocabulary words.

	Definition	Scrambled	Answer
1.	the passing of light through matter	SATRINMISSON	____________
2.	the transfer of energy carried by light waves to particles in matter	TIPABNOROS	____________
3.	the number of waves produced in a given amount of time	QUECENFRY	____________
4.	a lens that is thinner in the middle than at the edges	ONACCEV	____________
5.	the release of light energy by particles of matter that have absorbed extra energy	GICANSTERT	____________
6.	the bouncing back of a wave after it strikes a barrier or object	LEFTECRONI	____________
7.	a curved, transparent object that forms an image by refracting light	SLEN	____________
8.	the distance between one point on a wave and the corresponding point on the next wave	VATHELWENG	____________
9.	waves that do not require a medium	TICELOCATREMNEG	____________
10.	a lens that is thicker in the middle than at the edges	NEXVOC	____________
11.	disturbance that transmits energy through matter or space	VEAW	____________
12.	material that gives a substance its color by reflecting some colors of light and absorbing others	PNETGIM	____________
13.	the bending of a wave as it passes at an angle from one medium to another	CRATERFONI	____________

Name ____________________ Date ____________ Class ____________

CHAPTER 4

REINFORCEMENT WORKSHEET

An Ecosystem

Complete this worksheet after you finish reading Chapter 4, Section 1.
Examine the picture below. It shows living and nonliving things existing in an ecosystem. Fill in the table to describe the organization of this ecosystem.

Nonliving things	Populations

1. What makes up the community in this ecosystem?

____

____

____

____

Name ______________________ Date ____________ Class ____________

CHAPTER 4 REINFORCEMENT WORKSHEET

Building a Eukaryotic Cell

Complete this worksheet after you finish reading Chapter 4, Section 3.
Below is a list of the features found in eukaryotic cells. Next to each feature, write a *P* if it is a feature found only in plant cells and a *B* if it is a feature that can be found in both plant and animal cells.

1. ______ endoplasmic reticulum

2. ______ mitochondria

3. ______ nucleus

4. ______ vacuole

5. ______ cell membrane

6. ______ cytoplasm

7. ______ ribosomes

8. ______ Golgi complex

9. ______ cell wall

10. ______ vesicles

11. ______ DNA

12. ______ nucleolus

13. ______ chloroplasts

In the space provided, label the structures of the eukaryotic cell drawn below. Include all of the structures that you labeled *B*.

A Eukaryotic Cell

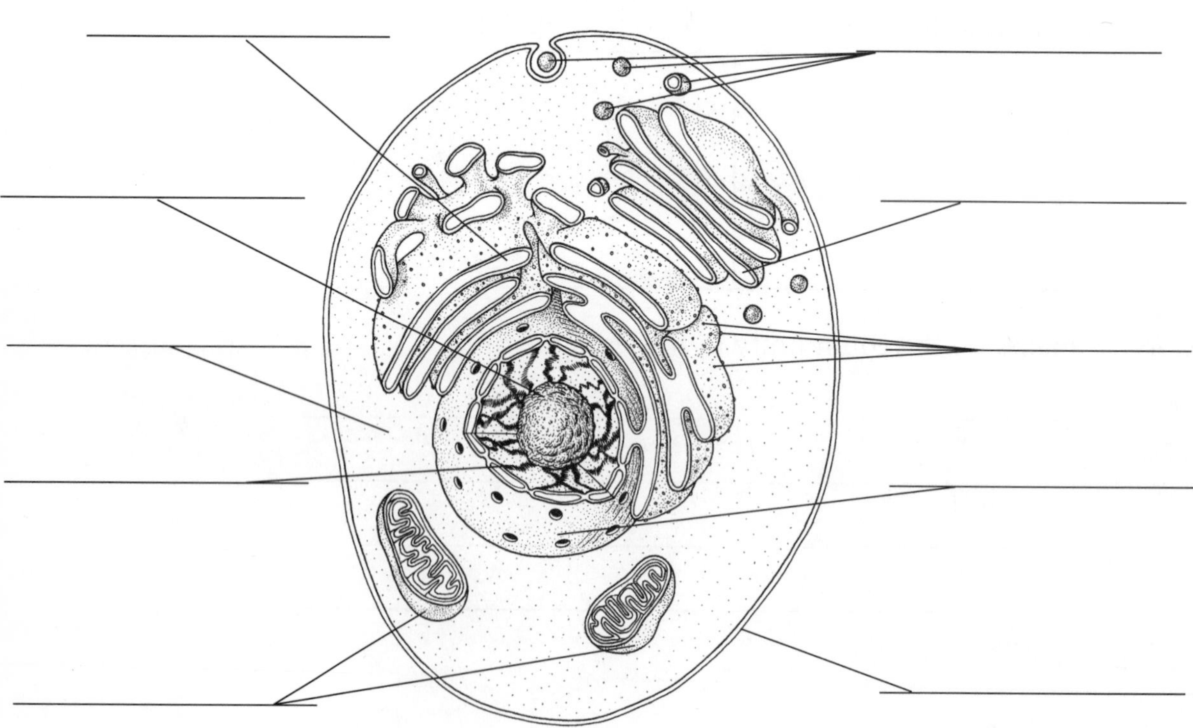

Name ______________________________ Date ______________ Class ______________

CHAPTER 4 **VOCABULARY REVIEW WORKSHEET**

A Cell Crossword Puzzle

Try this puzzle after finishing Chapter 4.
Use the clues below to complete the crossword puzzle on the next page.

ACROSS

1. The fluid inside a cell

6. Another name for 12 across

9. The control center of a cell

11. Special vesicles containing enzymes

12. Cells that do not have a nucleus

14. Organelle that modifies, packages, and transports materials out of the cell

18. Describes an organism that can exist only as a group of cells

22. A single ________ has all of the items necessary to carry out life's activities.

23. A combination of two or more tissues working together to perform a specific job in the body

25. British scientist who first observed cells under a microscope

26. Energy-converting organelle found in plant and algae cells

27. Anything that can live on its own

28. Groups of organs working together to perform particular jobs in the body

29. One of the structures a cell uses to live, grow, and reproduce

DOWN

1. All of the populations of different species that live and interact in an area

2. The cells of plants and algae have a hard ________ ________ made of cellulose.

3. Organelles where amino acids are hooked together to make proteins

4. The cell's hereditary material

5. A group of similar cells that work together to do a specific job in the body

7. Cells that have a central nucleus and a complicated inner structure

8. All eukaryotic cells have membrane-covered compartments called ________ that form when part of the cell membrane surrounds an object and pinches off.

10. A group of the same kind of organisms that live in the same area at the same time

13. The cell's power plants; break down food molecules to make ATP

15. Barrier between the inside of a cell and its environment

16. Dark spot inside the nucleus that stores the materials that will be used later to make ribosomes

17. Three statements that define all living things in terms of cells

19. The cell's delivery system (abbr.)

20. Special molecule that provides energy for a cell's activities

21. A community and all of the nonliving things that affect it

24. A large membrane-covered chamber that stores liquids and is found in plant cells

1
2
3
4
5
6
7
8
9
10
11
12
13
14
15
16
17
18
19
20
21
22
23
24
25
26
27
28
29

Name ______________________ Date ____________ Class __________

CHAPTER 5 REINFORCEMENT WORKSHEET

Into and Out of the Cell

Complete this worksheet after you have finished reading Chapter 5, Section 1.

Each of the boxes below represents a different method cells use to bring small particles into the cell or to take small particles out of the cell. Add the notes at the bottom of the page to the appropriate box. Be careful—some notes can be used more than once.

Small Particle Transport

Osmosis	Passive Transport	Active Transport

Notes

- particles move through protein doorways
- particles move through cell membrane between phospholipid molecules
- sugar or amino acids
- requires ATP
- particles move from an area of high concentration to an area of low concentration
- does not require ATP
- particles move from an area of low concentration to an area of high concentration
- water

Name ______________________ Date ______________ Class ____________

CHAPTER 5 REINFORCEMENT WORKSHEET

Activities of the Cell

Complete this worksheet after you have finished reading Chapter 5, Section 2.

1. Sketch and label a chloroplast and a mitochondrion in the space provided.

2. Chloroplasts use light energy during photosynthesis. To your drawing add a light source and an arrow from the light source to the chloroplast.
3. Chloroplasts give off oxygen and glucose during photosynthesis. Mitochondria use oxygen and glucose during cellular respiration. Add this information to your diagram.
4. During cellular respiration, mitochondria produce ATP. Add this information to your diagram.
5. Besides light energy, what do chloroplasts use to make glucose?

____

____

6. Besides ATP, what do mitochondria give off during cellular respiration?

____

____

7. Add the information from questions 5 and 6 to your diagram.

Name ______________________ Date ______________ Class ____________

CHAPTER 5

REINFORCEMENT WORKSHEET

This is Radio KCEL

Complete this worksheet after you have finished reading Chapter 5, Section 3.

Hello, Cell-O-Rama radio fans! Katy Chromosome here. We have a very exciting program in store for you: *Cell Mitosis in Action,* with local sports announcers Sid Toekinesis and Dee Ennay. To make this a Cell-O-Rama challenge, we've spliced the sound clips from each phase of mitosis in the wrong order. Your job is to identify the correct phase for each clip and then put the clips in the correct sequence. Good luck! Dee and Sid?

Sid: Thanks, Katy. Let's roll the tape, Dee.

Dee: Rolling . . .

Segment A: Mitosis Phase ____________

Sid: Dee, I think the Chromatid twins are really mad this time. They seem to be storming off in opposite directions. Don't they care about the game?

Dee: This is just incredible, Sid. Wait a minute! Both groups appear to be moving into huddles. Is the game over? Do you think they'll come back?

Segment B: Mitosis Phase ____________

Sid: Dee, this is UN-believable. The Chromatid twins are shrinking! Are they getting ready for a fight?

Dee: Sid, I am brand new to this game, and I just don't know what might happen next. Where on *Earth* are those centrioles going?

Sid: Dee, I think things are getting too hot for them. They are hightailing it out of there.

Dee: Oh no. They seem to be throwing a net to trap the Chromatid twins. It looks like the centrioles are herding them to the center of the field.

Segment C: Mitosis Phase ____________

Sid: This is truly amazing, Dee. Some sort of barrier seems to be forming around each of the huddles. What is going on?

Dee: Sid, believe it or not, I think the teams are taking a timeout. See how they're all unwinding? They have worked hard today. This has been *quite* a game!

Segment D: Mitosis Phase ____________

Sid: Dee, maybe they're getting ready for a kickoff. The twins are lining up along the center of the field. I think they're waiting for a signal.

Dee: Sid, you can just *feel* the tension in the air. Uh oh. I think a fight just broke out. Wait—they're all *wrestling* out there! The twins look like they're trying to get away from each other. Where are the refs when you need them?

Name ________________ Date ________ Class ________

CHAPTER 5

VOCABULARY REVIEW WORKSHEET

Cell Game Show

After you finish Chapter 5, give this puzzle a try!

This game may be played individually or in teams. You are supplied with the answers to questions in four categories. Your challenge is to come up with the correct question for each answer. Each correct "question" has a point value corresponding to the number at the beginning of the row. Keep a running total of your points as you play.

	To Make Two	On the Move	Lazy Days	I Can "C" You
50	These condense into an X-shape before mitosis.	How a cell membrane moves large particles into the cell	The movement of particles from an area of high concentration to an area of low concentration	This process ends when a cell divides and new cells are formed.
100	Human body cells have 23 pairs of these.	The movement of particles through proteins against the normal direction of diffusion	Oxygen can slip between these molecules, which make up much of the cell membrane.	This is the region where chromatids are held together.
200	Bacteria double this way.	This word means "outside the cell."	Diffusion of water across a membrane	The way organisms get energy from food using oxygen
500	The complicated process of chromosome separation; the second stage of the cell cycle	The process by which plants capture light energy and change it into food	The diffusion of particles through special "doorways" in the cell membrane	The cytoplasm splits in two during this process.
1000	During the third stage of the cell cycle, this forms in eukaryotic cells with cell walls.	When there's no oxygen for your cells, they use this to get energy.	Special doorways in the cell membrane are made of these.	Oxygen can pass directly through this cell part.

Total Points: ________

Name ______________________________ Date ______________ Class __________

CHAPTER 6 REINFORCEMENT WORKSHEET

Dimples and DNA

Complete this worksheet after you have finished reading Chapter 6, Section 1.

In humans, dimpled cheeks are a dominant trait, with a genotype of ***DD*** or ***Dd.*** Nondimpled cheeks are a recessive trait, with a genotype of ***dd.***

1. Imagine that Parent A, with the genotype ***DD,*** has dimpled cheeks. Parent B has the genotype ***dd*** and does not have dimpled cheeks.

   The Punnett square below diagrams the cross between Parent A and Parent B. Complete the Punnett square. (The first square has been done for you. You may want to refer to How to Make a Punnett square in your text.)

Parent A

Parent B

	D	D
d	Dd	
d		

2. A Punnett square shows what genotypes are possible for the offspring of a certain cross. What genotypes are possible for the offspring of Parent A and Parent B?

____

____

3. Each of the four squares of a Punnett square represents a 25 percent probability that the offspring will have that particular genotype. What is the probability that the offspring of Parent A and Parent B will have dimpled cheeks?

____

____

____

____

4. Parent X, with the genotype ***Dd,*** has dimpled cheeks. Parent Y also has the genotype ***Dd*** and has dimpled cheeks as well. To find out what their offspring might look like, complete the Punnett square below.

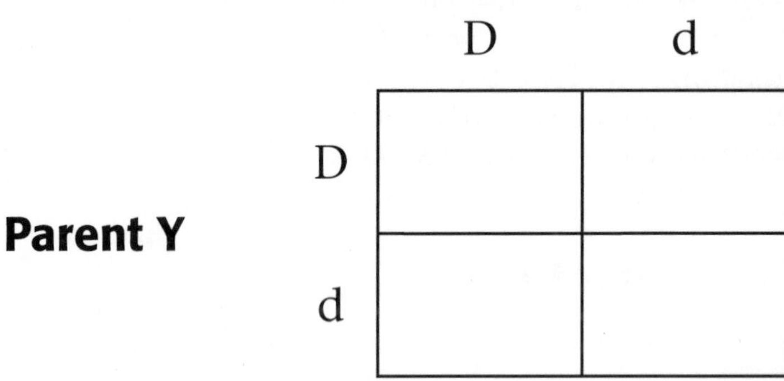

5. What is the probability that the offspring of Parent X and Parent Y will have each of the following genotypes?

DD: ______________________________

Dd: ______________________________

dd: ______________________________

6. What is the probability that the offspring of Parent X and Parent Y will have nondimpled cheeks?

____

____

____

7. What is the probability that the offspring of Parent X and Parent Y will have dimpled cheeks? (Remember that there are two genotypes that can produce dimpled cheeks.)

____

____

____

Name ______________________________ Date ______________ Class ___________

CHAPTER 6

VOCABULARY REVIEW WORKSHEET

Vocabulary Garden

After you finish Chapter 6, give this puzzle a try!

Write the word or phrase being described below in the appropriate space on the next page.

1. chromosomes with matching information
2. carry genes that determine the sex of offspring
3. the two genes that govern the same characteristic
4. an organism's inherited combination of alleles
5. nuclear division in eukaryotic cells in which each cell receives a copy of the original chromosomes
6. the passing of traits from parents to offspring
7. cell division that produces sex cells
8. kind of trait that seemed to vanish in the offspring produced in Mendel's first experiment
9. tool used to visualize all the possible combinations of alleles from parents
10. kind of trait that always appeared in the offspring produced in Mendel's first experiment
11. A true-________________ plant always produces offspring with the same trait as the parent(s).
12. A self-________________ plant contains both male and female reproductive structures.
13. male sex cells
14. an organism's inherited appearance
15. female sex cells
16. the mathematical chance that an event will occur
17. located on chromosomes and carry hereditary instructions

Name ______________________ Date __________ Class __________

Vocabulary Garden, continued

1. _ _ _ _ _ _ **G** _ _ _

2. _ _ _   _ _ **R** _ _ _ _ _ _ _ _

3. _ _ _ **E** _ _ _

4. **G** _ _ _ _ _ _ _

5. _ _ _ **O** _ _ _

6. _ _ **R** _ _ _ _ _

7. **M** _ _ _ _ _ _

8. _ _ _ **E** _ _ _ _ _

9. _ _ _ **N** _ _ _   _ _ _ _ _ _

10. **D** _ _ _ _ _ _ _

11. _ _ **E** _ _ _ _ _

12. _ _ **L** _ _ _ _ _ _ _ _

13. **S** _ _ _ _

14. _ _ _ _ _ _ _ **P** _

15. **E** _ _ _

16. _ _ _ _ **A** _ _ _ _ _ _

17. _ _ _ _ **S**

18. What do Gregor Mendel's peas have to do with the study of heredity?

____

____

____

____

____

____

Name ______________________________ Date ______________ Class __________

CHAPTER

7 REINFORCEMENT WORKSHEET

DNA Mutations

Complete this worksheet after reading Chapter 7, Section 2.

DNA is made up of nucleotides that each contain a sugar, a phosphate, and a base. The four possible bases are: adenine, cytosine, thymine, and guanine. Remember that adenine and thymine are complementary and form pairs, and cytosine and guanine are complementary and form pairs.

1. Below is half of a section of DNA that has been split apart and is ready to copy itself. Write the appropriate letter in the space provided to build the DNA's new complementary strand.

G - - - - - - - - - - ___
T - - - - - - - - - - ___
A - - - - - - - - - - ___
A - - - - - - - - - - ___
C - - - - - - - - - - ___
T - - - - - - - - - - ___
C - - - - - - - - - - ___
C - - - - - - - - - - ___
T - - - - - - - - - - ___

2. Sometimes mistakes happen when the DNA is being copied. These mistakes, or mutations, change the order of the bases in DNA. There are three kinds of mutations that can occur in DNA: deletion, insertion, and substitution.

a. Below are two sequences—an original sequence of bases in DNA and the sequence of bases after a mutation has occurred. On the original base sequence, show where the mutation has occurred by circling the appropriate base pair, and write what type of mutation it is in the space provided.

Base sequence in original cell DNA		Base sequence in a cell with mutated DNA		
C	G	C	G	
T	A	T	A	
C	G	C	G	
C	G	C	G	
T	A	T	A	
A	T	A	T	______________
A	T	A	T	
A	T	A	T	
C	G	T	A	
C	G	C	G	
T	A	T	A	

b. Below are two more sequences—an original sequence of bases in DNA and the sequence of bases after a mutation has occurred. On the original base sequence, show where the mutation has occurred by circling the appropriate base pair, and write what type of mutation it is in the space provided.

Base sequence in original cell DNA		Base sequence in a cell with mutated DNA	
C	G	C	G
T	A	T	A
A	T	A	T
C	G	C	G
C	G	C	G
G	C	G	C
T	A	T	A
A	T	A	T
A	T	A	T
G	C	A	T
A	T	T	A
T	A		

____

3. Ribosomes "read" a complementary copy of DNA in order to make proteins. Each group of three bases forms the code for an amino acid. When mutations occur in DNA, they can change the information that the DNA carries.

To understand this process better, look at the sentence below, which uses only three-letter words.

AMY GOT THE RED HOT POT OFF THE LOG

If one letter is deleted from this sentence, it becomes:

AMY GTT HER EDH OTP OTO FFT HEL OG

How is this similar to what can happen when a mutation occurs in DNA?

____

____

____

____

Name ______________________________ Date ______________ Class ____________

CHAPTER 7

VOCABULARY REVIEW WORKSHEET

Unraveling Genes

Try this puzzle after you finish reading Chapter 7!

Solve the clues and unscramble the letters to fill in the blanks. Fill the letters in the squares and read the final clue to unravel the secret message.

1. Molecule that carries our hereditary information: NAD

___ ___ ___
11

2. Subunits of DNA: DISTONEUCLE

___ ___ ___ ___ ___ ___ ___ ___ ___ ___ ___
1

3. Nucleotide base known as A: ENIDANE

___ ___ ___ ___ ___ ___ ___
16 14

4. Complement of question 3: TIEHYMN

___ ___ ___ ___ ___ ___ ___
5

5. Nucleotide base known as G: NUANIGE

___ ___ ___ ___ ___ ___ ___
15

6. Complement of question 5: YOSTINCE

___ ___ ___ ___ ___ ___ ___ ___
4

7. Shape of a DNA molecule (two words): EXELLIDOBUH

___ ___ ___ ___ ___ ___   ___ ___ ___ ___ ___
12 7

8. Organelle that manufactures proteins: MOOSERIB

___ ___ ___ ___ ___ ___ ___ ___
10

9. A change in the order of the bases of an organism's DNA: UNMATIOT

___ ___ ___ ___ ___ ___ ___ ___
13 17

10. Anything that can cause damage to DNA: UNGATEM

___ ___ ___ ___ ___ ___ ___
9

11. A tool for tracing a trait through generations of a family: DEEPGIRE

___ ___ ___ ___ ___ ___ ___ ___
6

12. Manipulation of genes that allows scientists to put genes from one organism into another organism: (two words) NEETIEGGINGECINNER

___ ___ ___ ___ ___ ___ ___
18

___ ___ ___ ___ ___ ___ ___ ___ ___ ___ ___

13. Analysis of fragments of DNA as a form of identification (two words): PANDINGINGFRENRIT

___ ___ ___   ___ ___ ___ ___ ___ ___ ___ ___ ___ ___ ___ ___ ___ ___ ___
(19)

14. Genes are located on these structures that are found in the nucleus of most cells: SHROCOMEMOS

___ ___ ___ ___ ___ ___ ___ ___ ___ ___ ___
(8)

15. DNA that results when genes from one organism are put into another organism using genetic engineering: BINRANTECOM

___ ___ ___ ___ ___ ___ ___ ___ ___ ___ ___
(3)

16. The goal of the Human ________ Project is to map the location and sequence of all our genes: MONEEG

___ ___ ___ ___ ___ ___
(2)

FINAL CLUE:

Occurs when different traits are equally dominant and each allele has its own degree of influence:

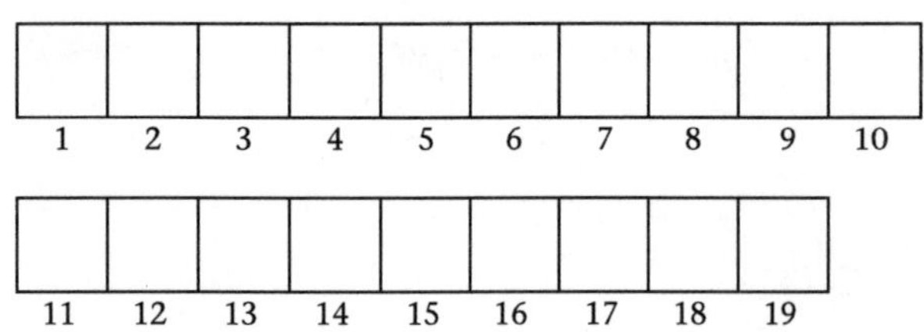

Name ______________________ Date ____________ Class ____________

CHAPTER

8 REINFORCEMENT WORKSHEET

Bicentennial Celebration

Complete this worksheet after reading Chapter 8, Section 2.

Imagine that it is 2059—the 200th anniversary of the publication of Darwin's *On the Origin of Species*. You are a reporter for a science magazine that is publishing a special issue about evolutionary biology. Your assignment is to write an article about Darwin, his travels, and his scientific theory of evolution. Include details about the Galápagos finches and how Darwin first got the idea for his theory, and explain the steps in the process of natural selection. Don't forget to give your article an eye-catching headline!

Name ______________________ Date ____________ Class ____________

CHAPTER

8 **VOCABULARY REVIEW WORKSHEET**

Charles Darwin's Legacy

After you finish Chapter 8, give this puzzle a try.
Unscramble each of the words below, and write the word in the space provided.

1. SISEPCE — a group of organisms that can mate to produce fertile offspring

2. CATEISPOIN — the process by which two populations become so different they can no longer interbreed

3. ASTRIT — distinguishing qualities that can be passed on from parents to offspring

4. SVELETICE — ________ breeding is the breeding of organisms that have a certain desired trait.

5. TAPATIDONA — a hereditary characteristic that helps an organism survive and reproduce in its environment

6. ALTRAUN — Successful reproduction is the fourth step of ________ selection.

7. GLEVITIAS — describes once-useful structures

8. SLOSFIS — solidified remains of once-living organisms

9. MAUTONTI — a change in a gene at the DNA level

Now unscramble the circled letters to find Darwin's legacy.

Name ______________________________ Date ____________ Class ____________

CHAPTER

9 REINFORCEMENT WORKSHEET

Earth Timeline

Complete this worksheet after you finish reading Chapter 9, Section 1.
Scientists use four major divisions to talk about the Earth's history: Precambrian time, the Paleozoic era, the Mesozoic era, and the Cenozoic era. Precambrian time lasted for about 88 percent of the 4.6 billion years of Earth's history. The Paleozoic era was about 6.3 percent of Earth's history. The Mesozoic era was about 4.0 percent of Earth's history. The Cenozoic era has lasted for about 1.4 percent of the Earth's history.

The Earth's history is difficult to imagine because it is so long. But what if the entire history of the Earth could fit into a single human life span of 80 years? Fill in the timeline below to show how old a person would be when each era begins. If the first single-celled organism appeared 3.5 billion years ago, how old would the person be when the first single-celled organism appears on Earth? Indicate this on the timeline.

Age in years

0
5
10
15
20
25
30
35
40
45
50
55
60
65
70
75
80

Name ______________________ Date ______________ Class ____________

CHAPTER 9 **REINFORCEMENT WORKSHEET**

Condensed History

Complete this worksheet after you finish reading Chapter 9, Section 2.
Many important events that have occurred since the Earth was formed are listed below. Fill in the diagram below, listing the events in chronological order.

Prokaryotes form.

Cells with nuclei form.

Began 65 million years ago

First birds appear.

Large mammals appear.

The ozone layer develops.

Dinosaurs dominate the Earth.

Plants become established on land.

Humans appear.

Crawling insects appear on land.

Many reptile species evolve.

Organisms suffer largest mass extinction known.

Small mammals survive mass extinction.

Began 540 million years ago

Cyanobacteria begin photosynthesis and produce oxygen.

Began 4.6 billion years ago

Winged insects appear.

Began 248 million years ago

Precambrian Time
Paleozoic Era
Mesozoic Era
Cenozoic Era

Name ______________________ Date ____________ Class ____________

CHAPTER 9

VOCABULARY REVIEW WORKSHEET

Mary Leakey's Search

Try this puzzle after you finish Chapter 9.
Solve each of the clues below, and write your answer in the spaces provided. Then complete the quotation by Mary Leakey on the next page by writing the letter that corresponds to each number in the empty boxes.

1. large mammals evolved during this era.

___ ___ ___ (5) ___ ___ ___ (6) ___ ___

2. scientist who uses fossils to reconstruct what happened in Earth's history

___ ___ ___ ___ ___ (8) ___ ___ ___ (10) ___ ___ ___ (33) ___ (31) ___ ___

3. measuring the ratio of unstable to stable atoms in a rock sample to estimate the age of the fossil it contains

___ (24) ___ (52) ___ ___ (28) ___ ___ (23) ___ ___   ___ (17) ___ ___ (48) ___ ___ ___

4. the first true cells

___ ___ ___ ___ (4) ___ ___ ___ (1) ___ (35) ___ ___ (53) ___

5. cells that contain a nucleus

___ ___ (9) ___ (30) ___ ___ ___ (42) ___ (56) ___ ___ ___

6. scientist who discovered fossilized footprints in Tanzania

___ ___ ___ ___ (13)   ___ (41) ___ ___ ___ (54) ___ ___ (7)

7. hominid that lived in Germany 230,000 years ago

___ (16) ___ ___ ___ ___ ___ ___ (37) ___ ___ (51) ___ ___

8. an imprint of a living thing preserved in rock

___ (14) ___ ___ ___ ___ ___ (12)

9. Lucy is the most complete example of a(n) ________ ever found.

___ ___ (3) ___ ___ ___ (36) ___ ___ ___ ___ ___ ___ ___ (18) ___ ___ ___ ___ (32) ___

10. When a species dies out completely, it becomes ________.

___ (38) ___ ___ ___ (15) ___ ___ ___ (20)

11. the theory that explains how the continents move

___ ___ (27) ___ ___ (50) ___   ___ ___ (47) ___ ___ ___ ___ (11) ___ ___ ___

12. a group of mammals with binocular vision and opposable thumbs

___ ___ ___ ___ ___ ___ ___ ___
(49 under blank 2; 45 under blank 6)

13. Humans and their humanlike ancestors are called ________.

___ ___ ___ ___ ___ ___ ___ ___
(46 under blank 1; 55 under blank 5)

14. organisms that don't need oxygen to survive

___ ___ ___ ___ ___ ___ ___ ___ ___
(39 under blank 3; 25 under blank 5)

15. a gas that absorbs ultraviolet radiation

___ ___ ___ ___ ___
(2 under blank 1; 57 under blank 4)

16. the single landmass that existed about 245 million years ago

___ ___ ___ ___ ___ ___ ___
(19 under blank 2; 26 under blank 6)

17. The first birds appeared during this era.

___ ___ ___ ___ ___ ___ ___ ___
(29 under blank 4; 43 under blank 7)

18. During this era, the first land-dwelling organisms appeared.

___ ___ ___ ___ ___ ___ ___ ___ ___
(40 under blank 3; 22 under blank 5)

19. the process by which one type of rock changes into another type of rock

___ ___ ___ ___   ___ ___ ___ ___ ___
(21 under blank 6)

20. the time it takes for half of the unstable atoms in a sample to decay

___ ___ ___ ___ - ___ ___ ___ ___
(34 under blank 4; 44 under blank 7)

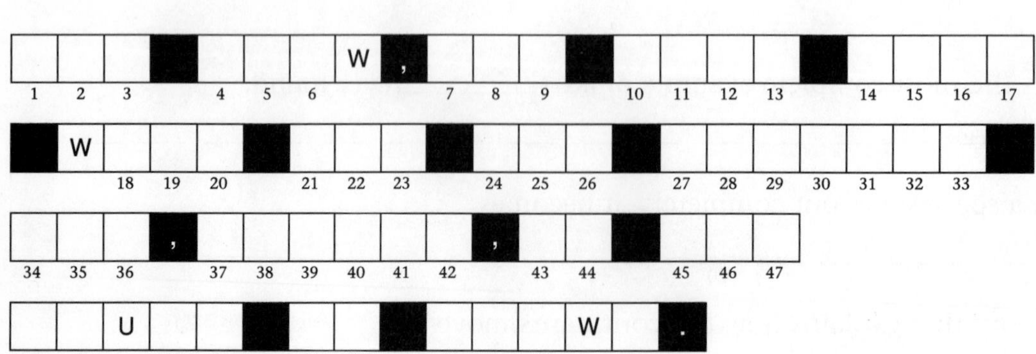

— Mary Leakey, 1994

Name ______________________ Date ____________ Class ____________

CHAPTER 10 **REINFORCEMENT WORKSHEET**

Keys to the Kingdom

Complete this worksheet after you have finished reading Chapter 10, Section 2.

Patty dropped her notes while she was studying the six kingdoms of living things, and now she isn't sure which facts belong to which kingdom. Each of the six boxes on the next page is labeled with the name of one of the kingdoms. Help Patty out by listing the facts, descriptions, and examples from Patty's notes below in the appropriate boxes. Be careful—some notes may fit in more than one kingdom.

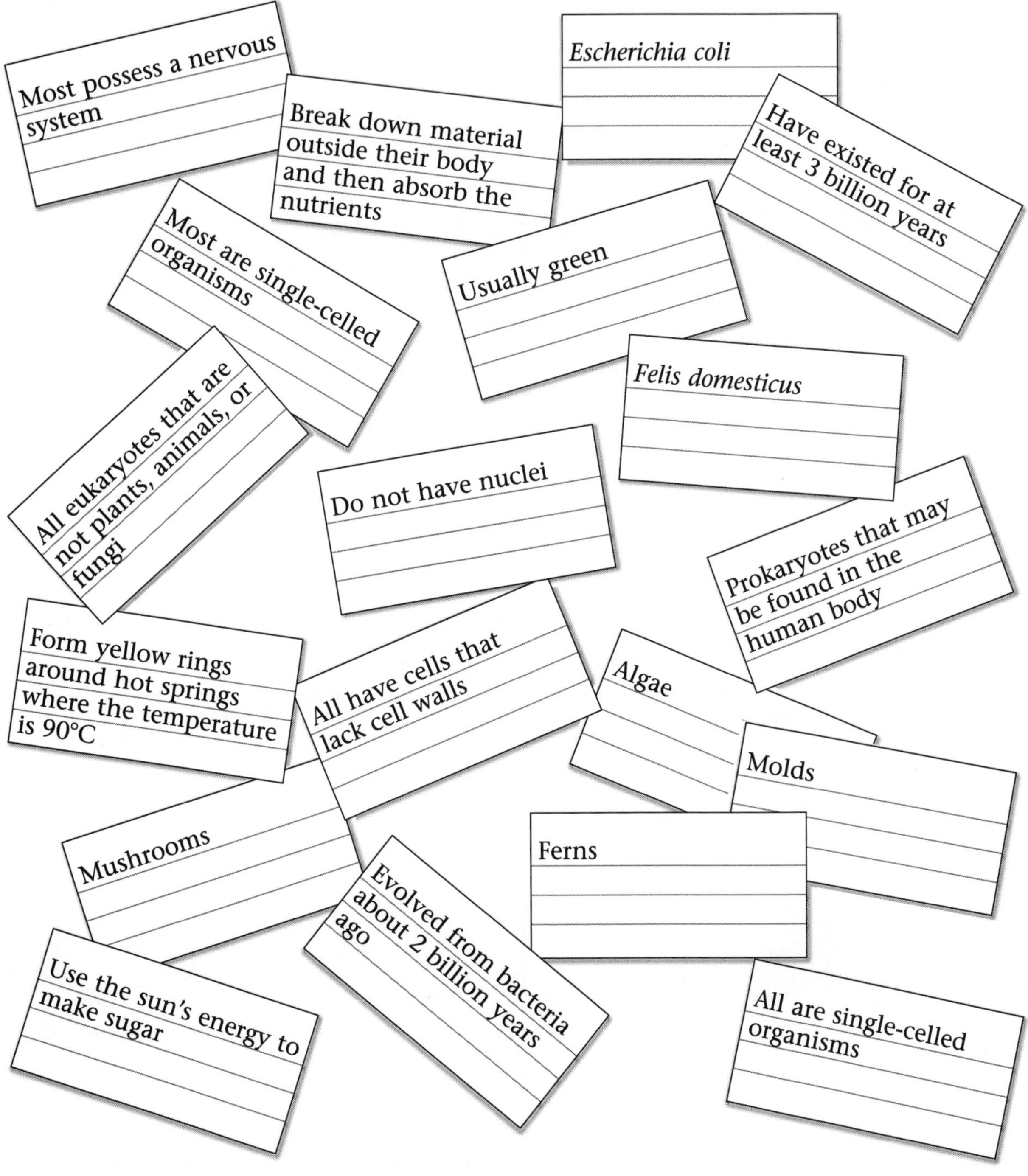

Name ______________________________ Date ______________ Class ____________

Animalia	Plantae
Protista	**Fungi**
Eubacteria	**Archaebacteria**

Name ______________________ Date ______________ Class ____________

CHAPTER 10 VOCABULARY REVIEW WORKSHEET

Classification Clues

Complete this puzzle after you have finished Chapter 10.

Solve the clues to see what words are hidden in the puzzle. Words in the puzzle are hidden vertically, horizontally, and diagonally.

1. List the seven levels used by scientists to classify organisms in order from most general to least general.

a. ______________________

b. ______________________

c. ______________________

d. ______________________

e. ______________________

f. ______________________

g. ______________________

2. For each of the following descriptions, write the kingdom of the organisms being described in the space provided.

a. ______________ Single-celled organisms without nuclei, such as *Escherichia coli,* which live in the human body

b. ______________ Multicellular eukaryotic organisms that are usually green and make sugar through photosynthesis

c. ______________ Unicellular prokaryotes that have been on Earth for at least 3 billion years

d. ______________ Multicellular organisms whose cells have nuclei but do not have cell walls

e. ______________ Multicellular organisms that have cells containing nuclei and that absorb nutrients from their surroundings after breaking them down with digestive juices

f. ______________ Single-celled or multicellular eukaryotic organisms that are not plants, animals, or fungi

3. Linnaeus founded ______________________, the science of identifying, naming, and classifying living things.

4. A ______________________ key is a special guide used to identify unknown organisms.

A	O	D	R	P	H	Y	L	U	M	X	O	B	K
M	R	I	O	K	N	A	R	I	P	P	H	Y	Y
O	E	C	M	R	E	H	O	C	M	L	Y	M	T
D	R	H	H	O	D	F	N	S	I	A	O	D	C
G	A	O	I	A	G	E	S	C	A	N	M	S	L
N	L	T	K	B	E	U	R	T	O	T	S	P	E
I	Q	O	I	U	N	B	E	X	S	A	U	E	U
K	H	M	Y	L	U	T	A	D	L	E	E	C	G
P	R	O	T	I	S	T	A	C	P	S	A	I	S
A	Y	U	T	I	E	B	D	R	T	E	R	E	F
I	L	S	G	U	V	O	G	U	C	E	H	S	O
Z	U	N	A	E	U	B	A	C	T	E	R	I	A
M	U	G	T	F	N	W	P	L	R	B	S	I	Y
F	A	M	I	L	Y	A	N	I	M	A	L	I	A

Name ______________________ Date ____________ Class ____________

CHAPTER 11 **REINFORCEMENT WORKSHEET**

Classifying Plants

Complete this worksheet after you finish reading Chapter 11, Section 3.

Each of the boxes below represents one of the main groups of living plants. Write the descriptions given at the bottom of the page in the appropriate box. Some descriptions may be used more than once.

Nonvascular plants	Vascular plants without seeds

Vascular plants with seeds but without flowers	Vascular plants with seeds and flowers

Notes

- ancestors grew very large
- conifers are an example
- provide land animals with almost all of the food they need to survive
- include the oldest living trees on Earth
- have rhizoids instead of roots
- angiosperms
- seeds are surrounded by a fruit
- are the most successful group of plants today
- mosses and liverworts
- usually the first plants to inhabit a new, bare environment
- formed fossil fuels
- ferns, horsetails, and club mosses
- gymnosperms
- must obtain water by osmosis
- contain xylem and phloem to transport water and food
- seeds develop in a cone or on fleshy structures attached to branches

Name ______________________ Date ______________ Class ____________

CHAPTER 11 **REINFORCEMENT WORKSHEET**

Drawing Dicots

Complete this worksheet after you finish reading Chapter 11, Section 3.

There are two classes of angiosperms—monocots and dicots. The main difference between the two classes is that monocots have one seed leaf and dicots have two seed leaves. However, there are other differences between them.

Below are illustrations of some of the features that distinguish monocots from dicots. Use the description of how a dicot differs from a monocot to draw the same features for a dicot.

Monocot	How is a dicot different from a monocot?	Dicot
Arrangement of vascular tissue	A monocot has bundles of vascular tissue scattered throughout the stem, while a dicot has bundles of vascular tissue arranged in a ring.	Arrangement of vascular tissue
Flower	A monocot has a flower with parts in threes, while a dicot has a flower with parts in fours or fives.	Flower
Pattern of leaf vein	A monocot has leaves with parallel veins, while a dicot has leaves with branching veins.	Pattern of leaf vein

Name ______________________ Date ____________ Class ____________

CHAPTER 11 **VOCABULARY REVIEW WORKSHEET**

Those Puzzling Plants

After finishing Chapter 11, give this puzzle a try!

Solve each of the clues below, and write your answer in the spaces provided.

1. spore-producing stage of a plant

___ ___ ___ ___ ___ ___ ___ ___ ___ ___(24)

2. plants with specialized tissue to move materials from one part of the plant to another

___ ___ ___(3) ___ ___ ___ ___ ___

3. male reproductive structure in a flower

___ ___ ___(12) ___ ___ ___

4. dustlike particles produced in the anthers of flowers

___ ___ ___ ___ ___(19) ___

5. small, hairlike threads of cells that keep mosses grounded

___ ___ ___ ___ ___ ___ ___(14) ___

6. openings in the epidermis of a leaf that let CO_2 into the leaves

___ ___ ___ ___ ___ ___(20) ___

7. plant "pipes" that transport sugar molecules

___ ___ ___ ___(2) ___ ___

8. waxy layer that coats the surface of stems and leaves

___ ___ ___ ___ ___ ___(18) ___

9. structures that cover immature flowers

___(5) ___ ___ ___ ___(26) ___

10. usually obtains water close to the soil surface

___ ___ ___(25) ___ ___ ___ ___   ___(9) ___ ___ ___

11. nonflowering, seed-producing plants

___ ___ ___ ___ ___ ___ ___ ___(8) ___ ___ ___

12. part of a flower that contains the ovules

___ ___ ___ ___(1) ___

13. seed leaf inside a seed

___ ___ ___ ___ ___ ___ ___(11) ___ ___(13)

14. attract pollinators to the flower

___ ___ ___ ___(22) ___ ___

15. outermost layer of cells that covers roots, stems, leaves, and flower parts

___ ___ ___ ___ ___ ___(7) ___ ___ ___

16. plants that have no "pipes" to transport materials from one part of the plant to another

___ ___ ___ ___(15) ___ ___ ___ ___(27) ___ ___ ___

17. seed-producing plants with flowers

___ ___ ___ ___ ___ ___ ___ ___ ___(23) ___ ___

18. plant "pipes" that transport water and minerals

___ ___ ___ ___(10) ___

19. can obtain water that is deep underground

___ ___ ___ ___ ___(17) ___ ___

20. plant stage that produces sex cells

___ ___(6) ___ ___(28) ___ ___ ___ ___ ___ ___ ___

21. tip of the pistil; collects pollen

___(21) ___ ___ ___ ___ ___

22. underground stem of a fern

___ ___ ___ ___ ___ ___ ___(4)

23. female reproductive structure in a flower

___ ___ ___ ___ ___(16) ___

Write the letter that corresponds to each number in the empty boxes to form the beginning of a well-known poem.

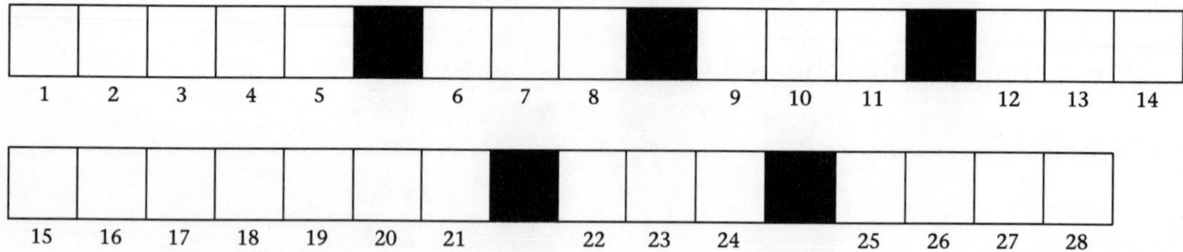

Name ________________________________ Date ______________ Class ___________

CHAPTER 12 **REINFORCEMENT WORKSHEET**

Fertilizing Flowers

Complete this worksheet after you finish reading Chapter 12, Section 1.

Flowers are adaptations that plants use for sexual reproduction.

1. Below is a cross section of a flower. Label the parts of the flower by writing each of the terms in the appropriate space.

TERMS

- sepal
- anther
- ovary
- pollen
- stigma
- style
- petal

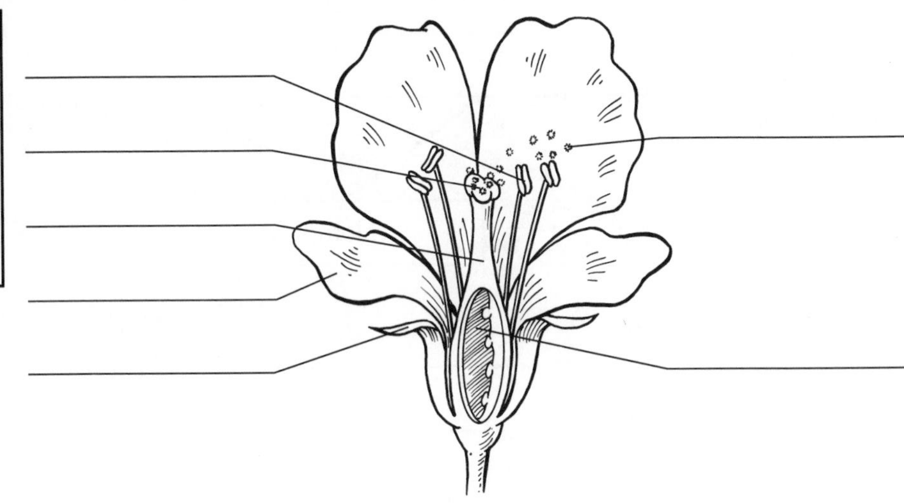

2. For fertilization to occur, a sperm has to reach the egg. Use the terms in the box below to label the following illustration, which shows how a sperm cell fuses with an egg in a flower.

TERMS

- egg within an ovule
- sperm cell
- pollen tube
- ovary

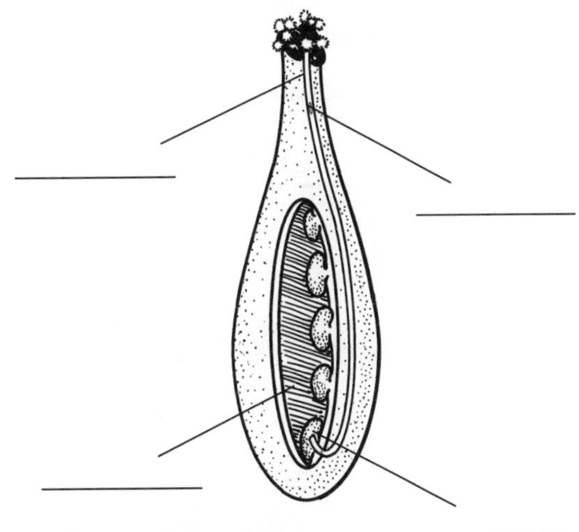

3. In the illustration above, which structure turns into the fruit after fertilization?

____

____

Name ______________________ Date ______________ Class ______________

CHAPTER 12 REINFORCEMENT WORKSHEET

A Leaf's Work Is Never Done

Complete this worksheet after you finish reading Chapter 12, Section 2.

A plant makes food in its leaves. Complete the outline below by filling in the blanks in the diagram with the words at the bottom of the page.

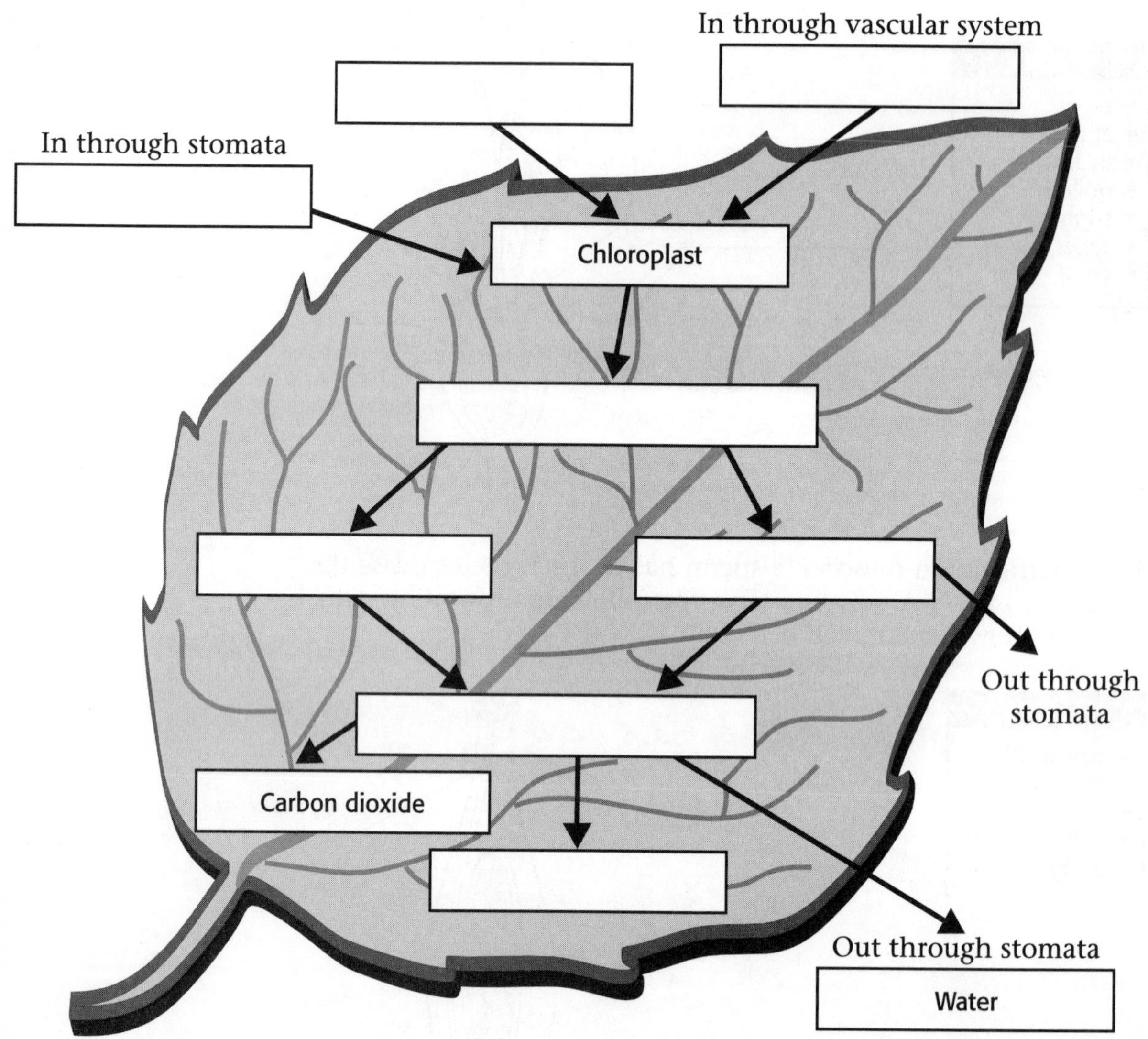

Words

- photosynthesis
- cellular respiration
- sugar
- carbon dioxide
- water
- oxygen
- sunlight
- energy

Name ______________________ Date ____________ Class ____________

CHAPTER 12 **REINFORCEMENT WORKSHEET**

How Plants Respond to Change

Complete this worksheet after you finish reading Chapter 12, Section 3.

Although plants don't walk and talk, they do respond to stimuli in their environment. Plants respond to stimuli by growing in a particular direction. Plant growth away from a stimulus is a negative tropism. Plant growth toward a stimulus is a positive tropism.

1. The plant shown below has just been moved next to a window from a room with no direct light. Sketch what the plant will look like in a few days.

In a few days

2. Phototropism is a change in the growth of a plant in response to light. Is phototropism positive or negative?

____

3. The plant shown below has just been tipped over on its side. Sketch what the plant will look like in a few days. (Hint: The plant will respond to gravity.)

In a few days

4. Gravitropism is a change in the direction of the growth of a plant in response to gravity. Is gravitropism of most shoot tips positive or negative?

____

Name ______________________ Date ____________ Class ____________

CHAPTER 12 VOCABULARY REVIEW WORKSHEET

Scrambled Plants

After you finish Chapter 12, try this puzzle!

Use the clues to unscramble each of the words below, and write the word in the space provided.

1. IOSDDUUEC — a tree that loses all of its leaves at the same time each year
2. TAOTSMA — the openings in a leaf's epidermis that allow carbon dioxide in and oxygen and water out
3. OISRMTP — a change in a plant's growth in response to a stimulus
4. NEREGEVER — a tree that keeps its leaves year-round
5. OORMHNE — a chemical messenger that carries information from one part of an organism to another
6. VAPMTGROSIIR — a change in the direction a plant grows in response to gravity
7. MOPTOPSIRHOT — a change in the way a plant grows in response to light
8. EUALCRLL EAPRRIINOST (two words) — the process that converts the energy stored in food into a form cells can use
9. AAIINNTTRRSPO — the loss of water from leaves
10. TRODNAM — inactive state of a seed

Now unscramble the circled letters to find the organelle that contains the photosynthetic pigment in plants.

Name ______________________ Date ______________ Class ____________

CHAPTER 13 REINFORCEMENT WORKSHEET

What Makes an Animal an Animal?

Complete this worksheet after reading Chapter 13, Section 1.

Whales, armadillos, hummingbirds, spiders… animals come in all shapes and sizes. Not all animals have backbones, and not all animals have hair. So what makes an animal an animal?

Complete the chart below by using the words and phrases at the bottom of the page.

Animal Characteristics

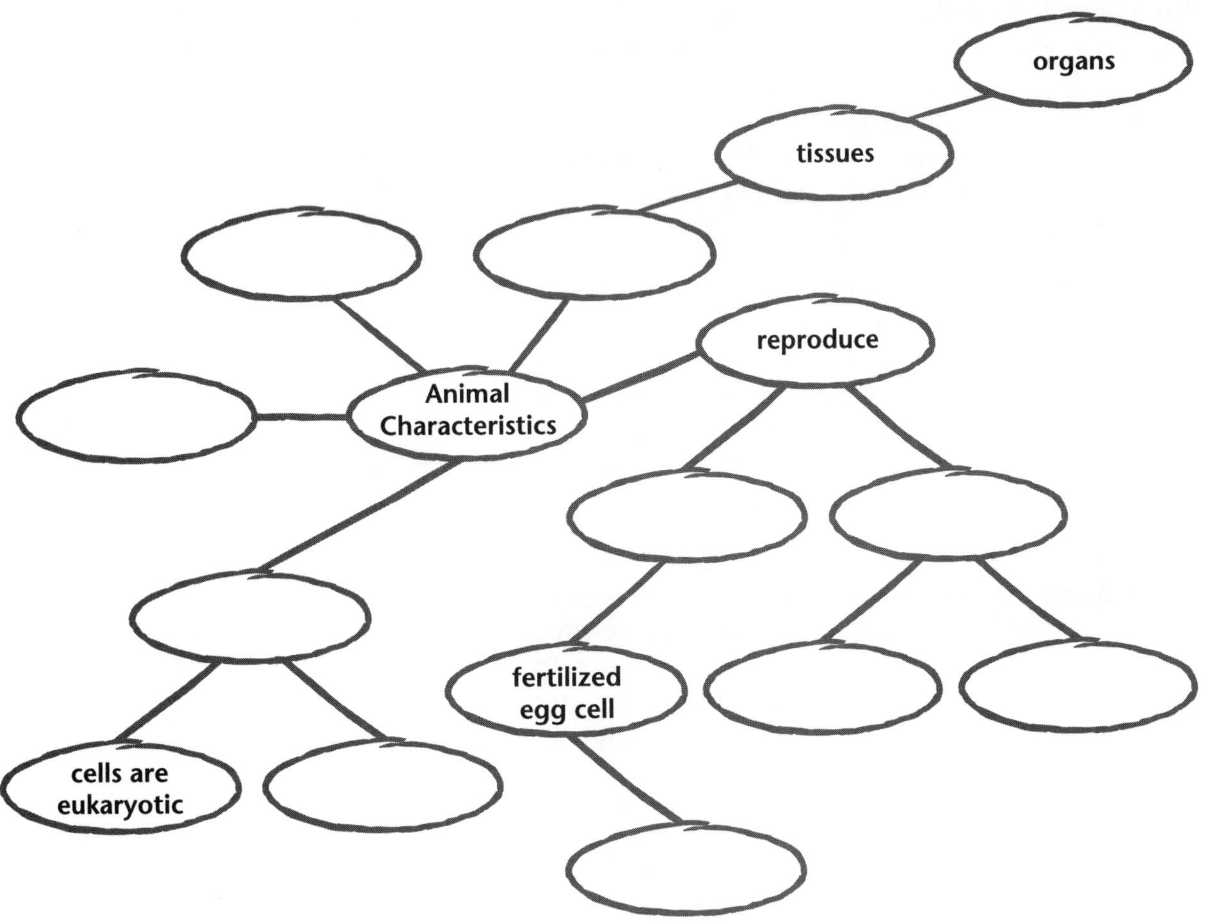

Words and Phrases

- move
- budding
- develop from embryos
- have specialized parts
- sexually
- asexually
- multicellular
- cells have no cell walls
- division
- are consumers

Name ______________________ Date ____________ Class ____________

CHAPTER 13 REINFORCEMENT WORKSHEET

Animal Interviews

Complete this worksheet after reading Chapter 13, Section 2.

Imagine that you work with Dr. Phishtof Finz, a researcher who can really talk to the animals. Below are some sections of his taped animal interviews. Your job is to decide what animal behavior or characteristic is being described and to write it in the space provided. Possible answers are *warning coloration, migration, hibernation, estivation,* and *camouflage.*

Interviewed animal		Behavior or characteristic
Canada goose:	During the summer, we stay up in Canada. It's really a nice place in summer, with lots of food and lots of sun. But before the snow starts to fly, we high-tail it south!	____________________
Arctic ground squirrel:	What's the winter like in Alaska? Strange, I really don't know. I spend all summer eating and getting my nest ready, but then during the fall I get so sleepy! I go to bed and—*poof!*—when I wake up it's spring!	____________________
Desert mouse:	Oh, living in the desert is wonderful! I love sunshine. During the really hot part of the summer, of course, I stay inside my nest, and I nap a lot. It's so much cooler inside.	____________________
Ladybug:	Thank you! I am a lovely shade of red, aren't I? But just between you and me, did you know that this beautiful color tells birds that I am, well, rather nasty tasting?	____________________
Chameleon:	Yoo-hoo! I'm over here! See? In the potted plant. Well, yes, I am rather proud of being able to turn that particular shade of green. Not all animals can do that, you know.	____________________

Name ______________________ Date ______________ Class ____________

CHAPTER 13 VOCABULARY REVIEW WORKSHEET

Puzzling Animal Behavior

After you finish reading Chapter 13, give this crossword puzzle a try! Solve the clues below, and write the answers in the appropriate spaces in the crossword puzzle.

ACROSS

3. to find one's way from one place to another

4. an organism that eats other organisms

6. this type of behavior can change item 17 down

7. an organism in the earliest stage of development

8. to travel from one place to another in response to the seasons or environmental conditions

10. an internal control of natural cycles

16. an area occupied by an animal or a group of animals from which other members of the species are excluded

18. this type of behavior is the interaction between animals of the same species

19. an animal that eats other animals

20. made of many cells

21. a period of inactivity that some animals experience in winter

DOWN

1. chemicals animals produce for communication

2. an animal without a backbone

5. coloration and/or texture that enables an animal to blend in with its surroundings

7. a period of reduced activity that some animals experience in summer

9. a collection of similar cells that work together to perform a specific job in the body

11. a combination of two or more of item 9 down

12. takes place when a signal travels from one animal to another and the receiver of the signal responds

13. fixed object an animal uses to find its way

14. ________ rhythms are daily cycles.

15. any animal with a skull and a backbone

17. behavior that is influenced by genes and does not depend on learning or experience

22. an animal that is eaten by another animal

Name ______________________________ Date ______________ Class ____________

Name ______________________ Date ____________ Class ____________

CHAPTER 14 **REINFORCEMENT WORKSHEET**

Life Without a Backbone

Complete this worksheet after you finish reading Chapter 14, Section 1.

What do a butterfly, a spider, a jellyfish, a worm, a snail, an octopus, and a lobster have in common? All of these animals are invertebrates. Clearly, there are many differences between these animals. Yet the most important characteristic these animals share is something none of them have—a backbone!

Despite their obvious differences, all invertebrates share some basic characteristics. Using the list of words provided, fill in the boxes with the correct answers. There will be some words that you will not use at all.

Characteristics

spicules
asymmetry
ganglia
gut
nerve cord
bilateral symmetry
collar cells
neutron
uniform
nerve networks
radial symmetry

All About Invertebrates

An invertebrate has a body plan that can have

____

____

____

An invertebrate might use these structures to digest its food.

____

____

An invertebrate might use one or more of the following structures to control its body movement.

____

____

____

Name ________________________________ Date ______________ Class ___________

CHAPTER

14 REINFORCEMENT WORKSHEET

Spineless Variety

Complete this worksheet after you finish reading Chapter 14, Section 4.

In each of the four completed lists, seven phrases were accidentally placed in the wrong list. Those seven phrases describe Annelid Worms. Circle the phrases that were placed incorrectly in the complete lists, and use those phrases to complete the list for Annelid Worms.

Echinoderms

live only in the ocean
have a brain
have an endoskeleton
have a nerve ring
are covered with spines or bumps
some have a radial nerve
have a water vascular system
sand dollar
sea urchin
a bristle worm

Annelid Worms

____
____
____
____
____
____
____

Arthropods

have a well-developed brain
have jointed limbs
have a head
have an exoskeleton
have a well-developed nervous system
a tick
an earthworm
a dragonfly

Mollusks

live in the ocean, fresh water, or land
have open or closed circulatory system
have a foot and a mantle
usually have a shell
have a visceral mass
have complex ganglia
a leech
a clam
a snail
have segments

Cnidarians

live in the ocean or fresh water
have a nerve cord
have a gut
have a nerve net
are in polyp or medusa form
have stinging cells
a jellyfish
a sea anemone
coral
have a closed circulatory system

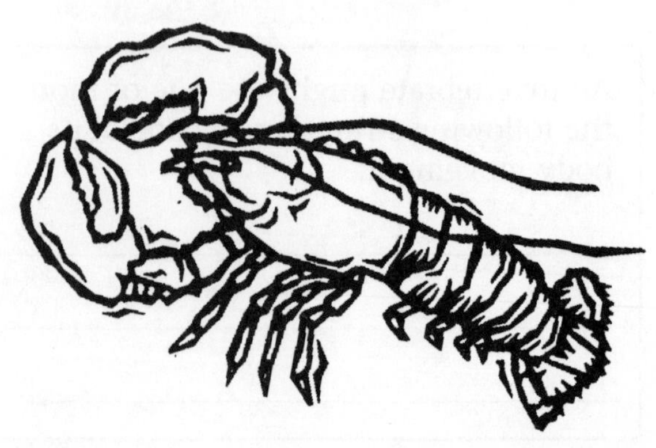

Name ________________ Date ________ Class ________

CHAPTER 14 VOCABULARY REVIEW WORKSHEET

Searching for a Backbone

After you finish Chapter 14, give this puzzle a try!

Identify the word described by each clue, and write the word in the space provided. Then circle the word in the puzzle on the next page.

1. external body-support structure made of protein and chitin ________________
2. combination of head and thorax ________________
3. type of circulatory system in which blood is pumped through a network of vessels that form a closed loop ________________
4. symmetry in which an organism's body has two halves that are mirror images of each other ________________
5. groups of nerve cells ________________
6. identical or almost identical repeating body parts ________________
7. form of cnidarian that looks like a mushroom with tentacles ________________
8. an animal without a backbone ________________
9. vase-shaped form of cnidarian ________________
10. type of circulatory system in which blood is pumped through spaces called sinuses ________________
11. the process through which an insect develops from an egg to an adult while changing form ________________
12. without symmetry ________________
13. three specialized parts of arthropods formed when two or three segments grow together
    a. ________________
    b. ________________
    c. ________________
14. symmetry in which an organism's body parts are arranged in a circle around a central point ________________
15. eye made of many identical light-sensitive cells ________________
16. pouch where almost all animals digest food ________________
17. jaws found on some arthropods ________________

18. the space in the body where the gut is located ______________

19. an organism that feeds on another organism, usually without killing it ______________

20. feelers that respond to touch or taste ______________

21. internal body-support structure ______________

22. organism on which the organism in item 19 lives ______________

23. system that allows echinoderms to move, eat, and breathe ______________

M	K	D	J	P	F	B	I	L	A	T	E	R	A	L	T	A
X	E	N	D	O	S	K	E	L	E	T	O	N	P	S	K	N
F	B	T	C	O	E	L	O	M	Y	E	P	V	O	E	X	T
P	A	G	A	A	S	U	D	E	M	L	E	H	F	T	M	E
I	Q	S	H	M	Z	O	W	A	Q	V	N	X	E	I	R	N
N	V	E	Y	K	O	D	A	N	I	P	A	X	J	S	A	N
V	G	L	L	M	P	R	E	A	G	R	O	N	S	A	L	A
E	X	B	N	X	M	M	P	M	O	S	Q	L	O	R	U	E
R	D	I	A	V	O	E	D	H	K	A	W	R	Y	A	C	F
T	L	D	W	D	B	N	T	E	O	B	P	X	G	P	S	S
E	A	N	B	A	P	O	L	R	D	S	A	R	A	M	A	E
B	S	A	O	C	L	E	J	E	I	R	I	W	N	S	V	G
R	E	M	P	A	T	G	S	G	O	C	P	S	G	U	R	M
A	D	E	H	O	B	O	X	H	U	K	A	X	L	N	E	E
T	A	P	N	X	L	Q	T	N	Z	T	S	L	I	V	T	N
E	E	J	P	C	O	M	P	O	U	N	D	O	A	Z	A	T
C	H	Z	G	F	R	I	L	A	I	D	A	R	T	U	W	S

Name ______________________ Date ____________ Class ____________

CHAPTER 15

REINFORCEMENT WORKSHEET

Coldblooded Critters

Complete this worksheet after you read Chapter 15, Section 4.

1. Take a look at each of the illustrations in the chart on the next page. Label each illustration "Reptiles," "Fishes," or "Amphibians."
2. Read over the characteristics listed below. Then on the next page, write each characteristic in the box next to the group of animals that commonly have that characteristic. Some characteristics may be used more than once.

consumers

thin, moist skin

ectotherms

external or internal fertilization

amniotic egg

many have scales

some have young born live

only internal fertilization

fins

gills

most lay eggs on land

metamorphosis

eggs laid in water

no scales

vertebrates

thick, dry skin

mostly external fertilization

breathe through skin and lungs

some have swim bladders

"double life"

lateral line system

breathe through lungs

some have skeletons of cartilage

many have bright colors to scare predators

almost all adults have lungs

Coldblooded Critter Chart

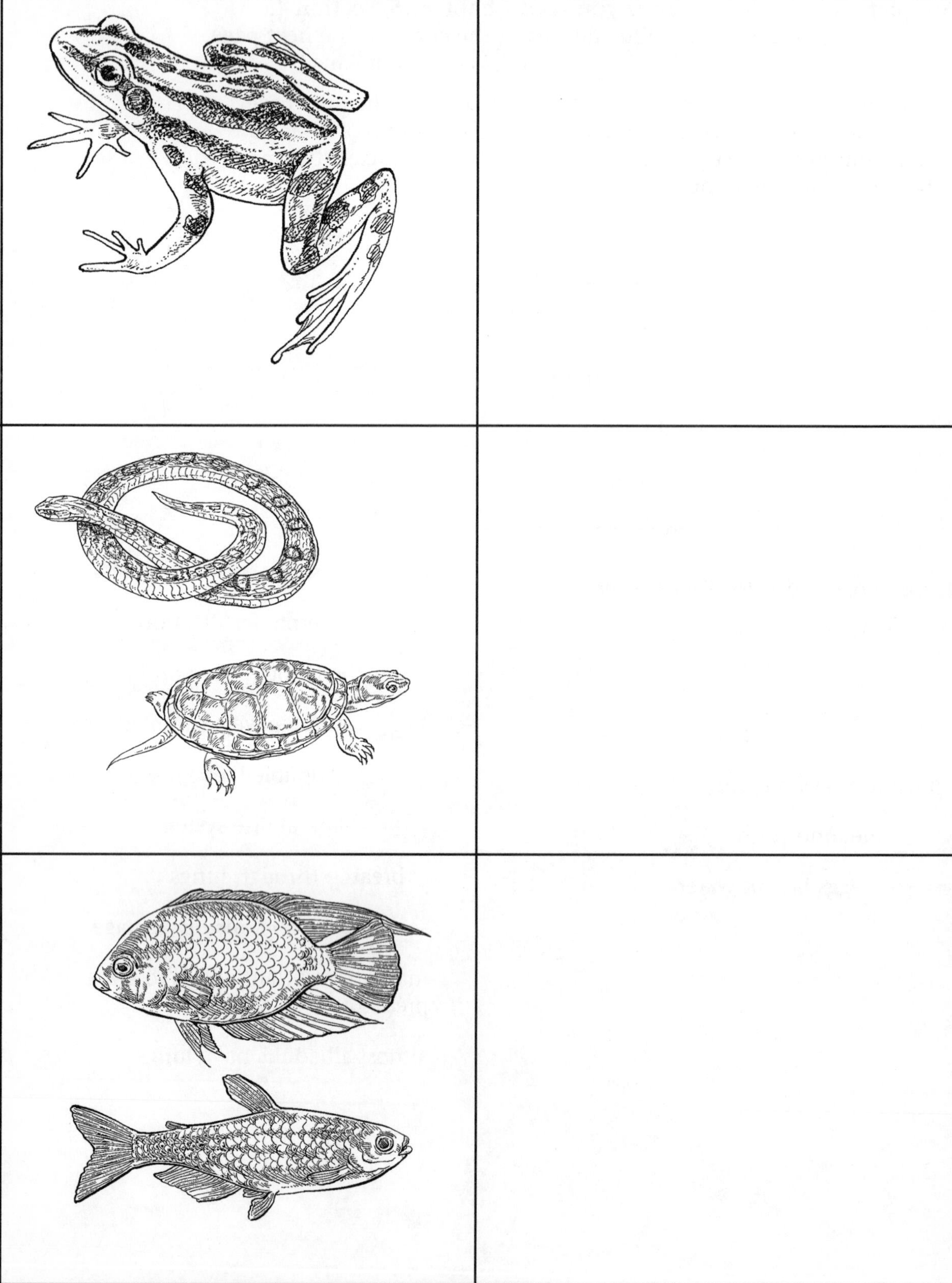

Name ______________________ Date ______________ Class ____________

CHAPTER 15 **VOCABULARY REVIEW WORKSHEET**

Fishin' for Vertebrates

Complete this puzzle after you finish reading Chapter 15.

ACROSS

1. crocodiles, turtles, and snakes

6. system of tiny rows of sense organs along the sides of a fish's body

8. cartilaginous fishes store oil here to stay afloat

9. group of fishes with skeletons made of bone and swim bladders

10. aquatic larva of an amphibian

11. balloonlike organ that gives bony fish buoyancy

14. an animal that maintains a constant body temperature

16. bony structures covering the skin of bony fishes

21. body parts of a fish that remove oxygen from water and carbon dioxide from blood

22. prehistoric reptile ancestor of mammals

23. frogs use a vocal sac to do this

24. structures made of bone contained in the fins of perch, minnows, and eels

25. hard-shelled reptiles that live only on land

DOWN

2. fertilization of an egg that occurs inside the female's body

3. fertilization of an egg that occurs outside the female's body

4. the first fishes were this type of fish

5. an animal with a body temperature that fluctuates with the temperature of its environment

7. an egg that is usually surrounded by a hard shell

12. small, toothlike structures on the skin of cartilaginous fishes

13. a change from a larval form to an adult form

15. sharks and skates are this type of fish

17. saclike organs that take oxygen from the air and deliver it to the blood

18. an animal with a skull and a backbone

19. these fishes have air sacs and can gulp air

20. fanlike structures that help fish move, steer, stop, balance

Name ____________________ Date ______________ Class ____________

Name ______________________ Date ____________ Class ____________

CHAPTER 16 **REINFORCEMENT WORKSHEET**

Mammals Are Us

Complete this worksheet after you finish reading Chapter 16, Section 2.

Each of the following terms is either an order of animals or an example of a particular order. Use the characteristics and facts in the table below to identify the order and one example of each group of animals, and record the corresponding terms in the spaces provided.

dolphin	cetaceans	hoofed mammals	sirenia
rabbit	human	carnivores	rodents
porcupine	aardvark	cow	toothless mammals
primates	manatee	Siberian tiger	
insectivores	lagomorphs	hedgehog	

Order	Characteristic	Example	An interesting fact
______	generally eat insects and have long, sticky tongues	______	only one is truly "toothless"
______	tend to have pointed noses for digging	______	live on all continents but Australia
______	small animals that have sharp front teeth for gnawing	______	front teeth never stop growing
______	have strong legs for jumping, sensitive noses, and big ears	______	some gather plants and shape them in "haystacks" to dry
______	have eyes that face forward and oppos-able thumbs	______	considered the most intelligent mammals
______	eat mostly meat	______	some handle food like monkeys do
______	generally fast runners; they have flat teeth for chewing plants	______	divided into groups according to the number of toes
______	water-dwelling mammals that resemble fish	______	use echolocation like bats do
______	eat seaweed and water plants	______	only four species in this order

Name ______________________________ Date ______________ Class ____________

CHAPTER 16 VOCABULARY REVIEW WORKSHEET

Is It a Bird or a Mammal?

Complete this worksheet after you finish reading Chapter 16.
Match each description in the second column with the correct term in the first column, and write the corresponding letter in the space provided.

_____ **1.** primates

_____ **2.** contour feathers

_____ **3.** carnivores

_____ **4.** down feathers

_____ **5.** gestation period

_____ **6.** preening

_____ **7.** placenta

_____ **8.** lift

_____ **9.** placental mammals

_____ **10.** brooding

_____ **11.** marsupials

_____ **12.** precocial chicks

_____ **13.** monotremes

_____ **14.** altricial chicks

_____ **15.** therapsids

_____ **16.** mammary glands

_____ **17.** diaphragm

a. a large muscle at the bottom of the ribcage that helps bring air into the lungs.

b. a mammal that nourishes its unborn offspring with a special organ inside a uterus

c. the time during which an embryo develops within the mother

d. a group of mammals that have opposable thumbs and binocular vision; includes humans, apes, and monkeys

e. chicks that hatch weak, naked, and helpless

f. a special organ of exchange that provides a developing fetus with nutrients and oxygen

g. mammals that lay eggs

h. prehistoric reptile ancestors of mammals

i. consumers that eat animals

j. feathers made of a stiff central shaft with many side branches called barbs

k. fluffy, insulating feathers that lie next to a bird's body

l. glands that secrete a nutritious fluid called milk

m. the upward pressure on the wing of a bird that keeps a bird in the air

n. when a bird uses its beak to spread oil on its feathers

o. chicks that hatch fully active

p. when a bird sits on its eggs until they hatch

q. a mammal that gives birth to partially developed, live young that develop inside the mother's pouch or skin fold

Name ______________________ Date ______________ Class ____________

CHAPTER 17 REINFORCEMENT WORKSHEET

Know Your Biomes

Complete this worksheet after you have finished reading Chapter 17, Section 1.

1. Using the Temperature & rainfall column as a guide, label the biomes using the following terms: *desert, tropical rain forest, arctic tundra, coniferous forest, temperate grassland, savanna,* and *temperate deciduous forest.*
2. Use the examples and characteristics given in the box on the next page to fill in the appropriate blanks.

Type of biome	Temperature & rainfall	Examples & characteristics
______________	summer: 38°C winter: 7°C rain: less than 25 cm per year	jack rabbit ______________ ______________
______________	dry season: 34°C wet season: 16°C rain: 150 cm per year	has scattered clumps of trees ______________ ______________
______________	daytime: 34°C nighttime: 20°C rain: up to 400 cm per year	the most biologically diverse biome ______________ ______________
______________ ______________	summer: 28°C winter: 6°C rain: 75–125 cm per year	woody shrubs beneath tree layer ______________ ______________

Name ______________________ Date ____________ Class ____________

Know Your Biomes, continued

Type of biome	Temperature & rainfall	Examples & characteristics
______________	summer: 12°C winter: −26°C rain: 30–50 cm per year	has no trees ______________ ______________
______________	summer: 14°C winter: −10°C rain: 35–75 cm per year	waxy coating on needles ______________ ______________
______________	summer: 30°C winter: 0°C rain: 25–75 cm per year	has few slow-growing plants ______________ ______________

EXAMPLES AND CHARACTERISTICS

musk ox
bison
giraffe
woodpecker
porcupine
animals prefer life in the treetops
most animals are active at night
trees produce seeds in cones
very few trees
plants spaced far apart
permafrost
trees lose leaves in fall
diverse groups of herbivores live here
most nutrients in the vegetation

Name ______________________ Date ____________ Class __________

CHAPTER 17

VOCABULARY REVIEW WORKSHEET

Eco-Puzzle

After you finish Chapter 17, give this puzzle a try!

In the space provided, write the term described by the clue. Then find those words in the puzzle. Terms can be hidden in the puzzle vertically, horizontally, or diagonally.

1. a biome in the far north where no trees can grow
____
2. a tree that produces seeds in a cone ______________________
3. soil that is always frozen ______________________
4. a hot, dry biome that receives less than 25 cm of rain a year
____
5. the zone of a lake or pond closest to the edge of the land
____
6. a treeless wetland ecosystem ______________________
7. microscopic photosynthetic organisms in the ocean
____
8. geographic area characterized by certain types of plants and animals ______________________
9. trees that lose their leaves in the fall
____
10. a wetland ecosystem with trees ______________________
11. an algae that forms rafts in the Sargasso Sea
____
12. an area where fresh and salty waters constantly mix
____
13. land where the water level is near or above the surface of the ground for most of the year ______________________
14. very small consumers in the ocean ______________________
15. a tropical grassland with scattered clumps of trees
____
16. a small stream or river that flows into a larger one
____
17. nonliving factors in the environment
____

18. a measure of the number of species an area contains

____

T	S	O	N	O	D	E	S	E	R	T	A	R	I	N	Z	X
U	V	C	W	T	R	I	B	U	E	Z	P	C	H	O	V	G
N	B	Q	E	F	E	G	C	L	L	I	T	T	O	R	A	L
D	L	S	T	S	O	R	F	A	M	R	E	P	Q	U	L	B
R	H	A	L	P	E	M	A	F	P	O	L	N	B	K	S	C
A	O	V	A	R	C	X	S	A	R	A	O	J	T	W	G	F
P	Y	D	N	D	V	F	J	C	N	T	G	O	A	Y	E	D
H	R	I	D	E	A	R	W	K	K	Y	N	M	C	M	H	S
Y	A	V	R	C	L	S	T	N	B	L	P	Z	O	X	L	A
T	U	E	M	I	Q	O	A	G	Q	C	I	I	N	K	Z	N
O	T	R	Y	D	N	L	P	R	M	O	B	T	I	R	O	N
P	S	S	C	U	P	I	B	E	G	K	F	V	F	Q	O	A
Z	E	I	Q	O	M	W	E	T	L	A	T	B	E	J	P	V
A	G	T	T	U	N	D	L	F	D	O	S	G	R	L	L	A
I	W	Y	R	S	C	I	T	O	I	B	A	S	O	N	B	S
V	H	E	A	B	M	A	R	S	H	N	D	L	U	W	T	E
P	D	J	L	C	Y	R	A	T	U	B	I	R	T	M	N	V

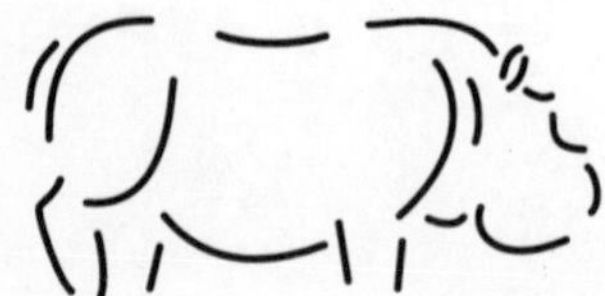

Name ______________________ Date ____________ Class ____________

CHAPTER 18 REINFORCEMENT WORKSHEET

It's "R" Planet!

Complete this worksheet after you finish reading Chapter 18, Section 2.

Use terms, definitions, and conservation suggestions from the lists below to design a flier that will encourage students in your school to participate in conservation. Get students' attention by making your flier colorful, using a catch phrase, or by using any other method you can think of. Your job is to make other students aware of the role they can play in protecting our environment. There's a sample flier on the next page.

- the three R's: reduce, reuse, recycle
- conservation: preserving resources
- recycling: breaking down trash in order to use it again
- resource recovery: turning garbage into electricity

- maintain biodiversity
- protect endangered species
- protect habitats
- enforce the Endangered Species Act

- to reduce means to use less
- to reuse means to use it again
- to recycle is a type of reuse

- plastics
- paper products
- waste wood
- glass
- cardboard
- cans

- use cloth napkins
- walk, ride a bike, or use public transportation
- use rechargeable batteries
- turn off lights, CD players, and computers when not in use

Do you want MORE out of life?

Get it by using less!! Here's how ...

REDUCE!

- **U**se a cloth napkin instead of a paper one.
- **U**se rechargeable batteries.

REUSE!

- **R**euse your plastic grocery bags.
- **G**ive away your old clothes.

RECYCLE!

- **Y**ou can recycle glass, cans, and cardboard, just to name a few.
- **P**urchase recycled products when you have the option.

It's "R" planet!
It's "R" responsibility to conserve!
"R" you??

Name ______________________________ Date ______________ Class __________

CHAPTER

18 VOCABULARY REVIEW WORKSHEET

Solve the Environmental Puzzle

Give this puzzle a try after you finish Chapter 18.

Using each of the clues below, fill in the letters of the term described in the blanks provided on the next page.

1. can be broken down by the environment
2. process of transforming garbage into electricity
3. type of hazardous wastes that take hundreds or thousands of years to become harmless
4. when the number of individuals becomes so large that they can't get all the resources they need
5. the process of making new products from reprocessed used products
6. the clearing of forest lands
7. the world around us
8. an organism that makes a home for itself in a new place
9. harmful substances in the environment
10. a girl who developed a way to make paper without cutting down a tree
11. describes a natural resource that can be used and replaced over a relatively short time
12. describes a natural resource that cannot be replaced or can be replaced only after thousands or millions of years
13. substances used to kill crop-destroying insects
14. the preservation of resources
15. the number and variety of living things
16. poisonous
17. the presence of harmful substances in the environment
18. protective layer of the atmosphere destroyed by CFCs

Name ______________________________ Date ______________ Class ______________

Solve the Environmental Puzzle, continued

1. ___ ___ ___ ___ ___ ___ **R** ___ ___ ___ ___ ___ ___

2. ___ ___ ___ ___ ___ ___ ___ ___   ___ **E** ___ ___ ___ ___ ___ ___

3. ___ ___ **D** ___ ___ ___ ___ ___ ___ ___ ___

4. ___ ___ ___ ___ ___ ___ ___ **U** ___ ___ ___ ___ ___ ___

5. ___ ___ **C** ___ ___ ___ ___ ___ ___

6. ___ ___ ___ ___ ___ **E** ___ ___ ___ ___ ___ ___ ___

7. ___ ___ ___ ___ **R** ___ ___ ___ ___ ___ ___

8. ___ ___ ___ **E** ___

9. ___ ___ ___ ___ **U** ___ ___ ___ ___ ___

10. ___ ___ ___ ___ ___   ___ ___ ___ ___ ___ ___ **S** ___

11. ___ ___ ___ **E** ___ ___ ___ ___ ___

12. ___ ___ ___ **R** ___ ___ ___ ___ ___ ___ ___ ___

13. ___ **E** ___ ___ ___ ___ ___ ___ ___ ___

14. **C** ___ ___ ___ ___ ___ ___ ___ ___ ___ ___ ___

15. ___ ___ ___ ___ ___ ___ ___ ___ ___ ___ ___ **Y**

16. ___ ___ ___ ___ **C**

17. ___ ___ **L** ___ ___ ___ ___ ___

18. ___ ___ ___ ___ **E**

Name ______________________ Date ______________ Class ____________

CHAPTER

19 REINFORCEMENT WORKSHEET

The Hipbone's Connected to the . . .

Complete this worksheet after you finish reading Chapter 19, Section 2.

Your skeleton makes it possible for you to move. It provides your organs with protection, stores minerals, makes white and red blood cells, and supports your body. Look at the human skeleton below, and write the names of the major bones listed below in the spaces provided.

Bones

- humerus
- fibula
- pelvic girdle
- radius
- patella
- ulna
- ribs
- skull
- clavicle
- vertebral column
- femur
- tibia

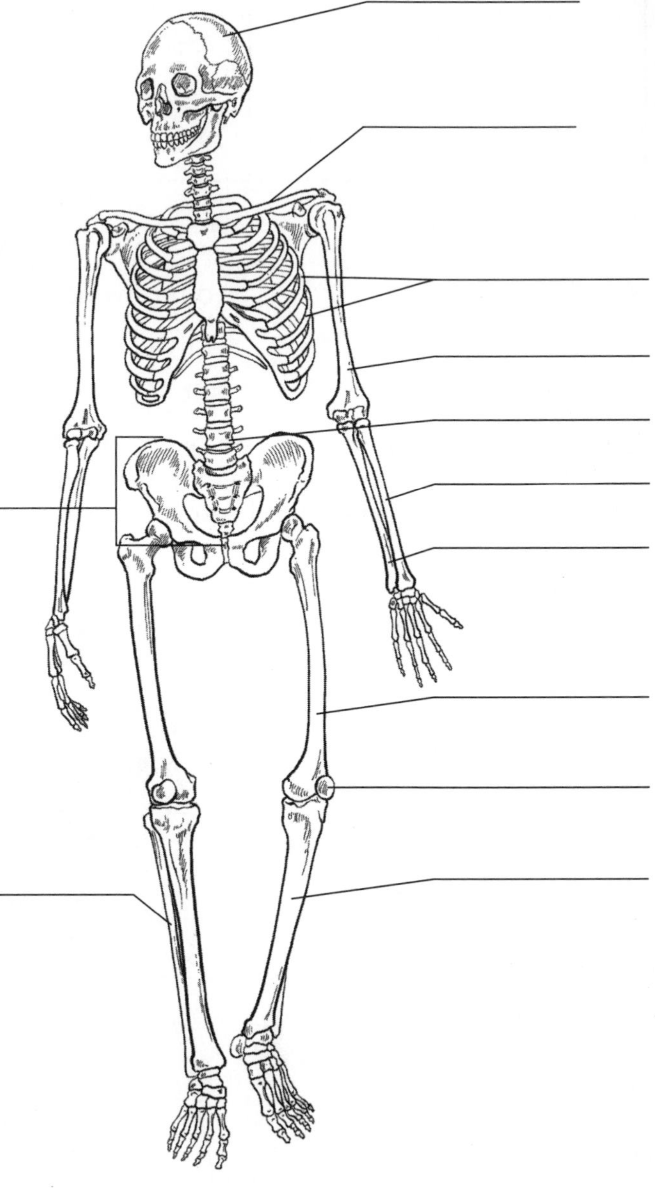

The place where two or more bones connect is called a joint. In the chapter, you looked at fixed, ball-and-socket, and hinge joints.

1. What kind of joint is the elbow?

____

____

2. What kind of joint allows the arm to move freely in all directions?

____

____

____

____

Name ______________________ Date ____________ Class ____________

CHAPTER 19

REINFORCEMENT WORKSHEET

Muscle Map

Complete this worksheet after you finish reading Chapter 19, Section 3.

Each of the boxes below represents one of the three types of muscle tissue in your body. Write the notes in the appropriate box. Some of the notes can be used more than once.

Three Types of Muscle

Skeletal	Cardiac	Smooth

Notes

- moves bones
- involuntary
- voluntary
- often works in pairs
- in the heart
- in blood vessels
- in the digestive tract

Look at the diagram of a human leg below. A flexor is a muscle that bends a part of your body when it contracts, and an extensor is a muscle that extends a part of your body when it contracts. Label the flexor muscle and the extensor muscle on the diagram below.

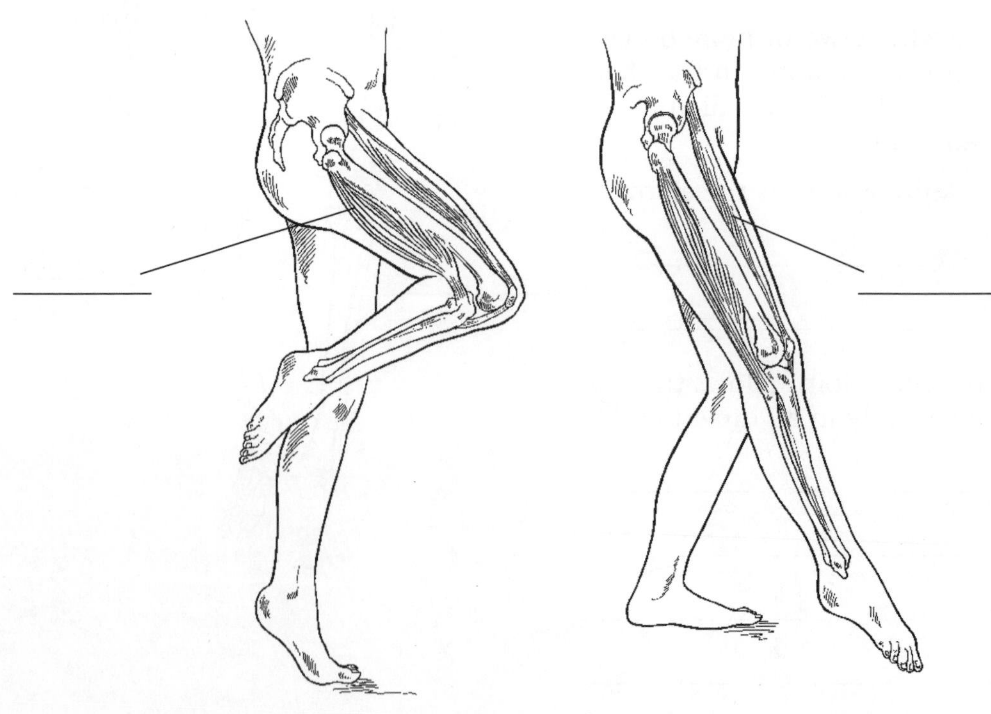

Name ______________________ Date ____________ Class ____________

CHAPTER 19 VOCABULARY REVIEW WORKSHEET

A Connective Crossword

Give this crossword puzzle a try after you finish reading Chapter 19!

Solve the clues below, and write the answers in the appropriate spaces in the crossword puzzle.

ACROSS

3. ________ is the type of bone tissue that gives a bone its strength. (two words)

8. place where two or more bones connect

10. small organs that produce a salty liquid that flows to the surface of the skin (two words)

11. ________ is the type of bone tissue that contains marrow. (two words)

17. Your ________ is made up of your skin, hair, and nails. (two words)

21. strong elastic bands of connective tissue that keep joints together

22. small organs in the dermis that produce hair (two words)

23. a group of similar cells working together

24. ________ is the type of tissue made of cells that contract and relax to produce movement. (two words)

25. ________ tissue sends electrical signals through the body.

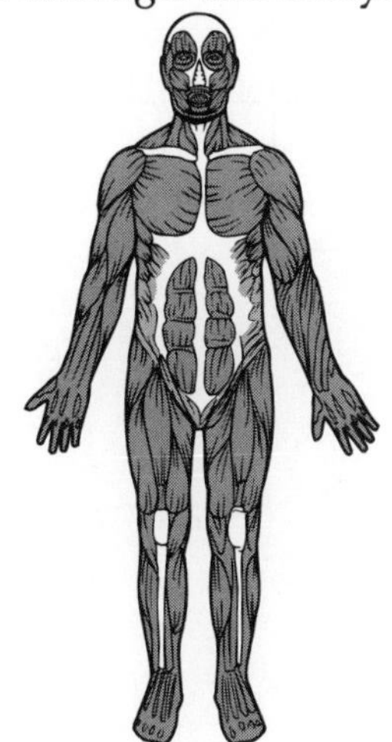

DOWN

1. two or more tissues working together

2. soft, flexible tissue that is found in the tip of your nose

3. ________ is the type of tissue that joins, supports, protects, insulates, and cushions organs. (two words)

4. the thin, outermost layer of skin

5. a muscle that straightens a body part

6. maintenance of a stable internal environment

7. strands of tough connective tissue that connect skeletal muscles to bones

9. ________ is found in the digestive tract and blood vessels. (two words)

12. ________ is the type of tissue that covers and protects underlying tissue. (two words)

13. a muscle that bends a body part

14. ________ muscle is found only in the heart.

15. thick layer of skin found under item 4 down

16. a collection of organs whose primary function is movement (two words)

18. ________ are muscles that move bones. (two words)

19. made up of bones, cartilage, and the special structures that connect them (two words)

20. a darkening chemical in skin that determines skin color

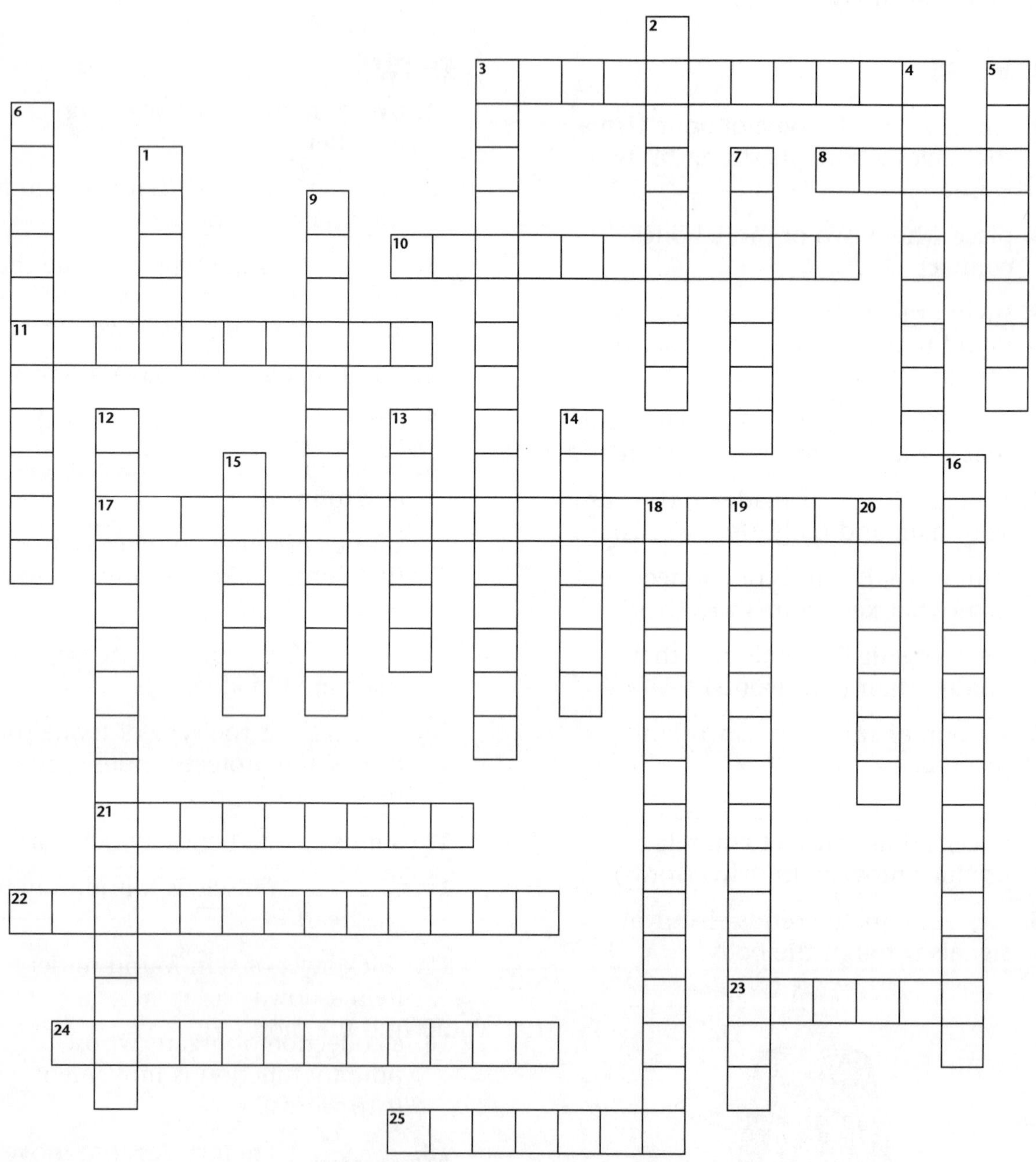
1
2
3
4
5
6
7
8
9
10
11
12
13
14
15
16
17
18
19
20
21
22
23
24
25

Name ______________________ Date ______________ Class ____________

CHAPTER 20 REINFORCEMENT WORKSHEET

Matchmaker, Matchmaker

Complete this worksheet after you finish reading Chapter 20, Section 1.

As you learned in this chapter, different blood types have different antigens and antibodies. Antigens are chemicals on the surface of red blood cells. Antibodies are chemicals in the blood's plasma. A person makes antibodies against the antigens that their red blood cells do not have. Those antibodies will attack any red blood cell that has those antigens, causing the red blood cells to clump together.

Antigens and Antibodies Present in Blood Types

Blood type	Antigens	Antibodies
O	none	A, B
A	A	B
B	B	A
AB	A, B	none

A person can receive blood from another person if the donor's blood does not contain antigens that the antibodies of the receiver's blood will attack. Complete the table below by writing *yes* or *no* in each of the blanks.

Receiver's blood type	Can receive type O?	Can receive type A?	Can receive type B?	Can receive type AB?
O				
A				
B				
AB				

1. Which blood type do you think a hospital would find the most useful? Explain.

____

____

____

____

Name ______________________ Date ______________ Class ____________

CHAPTER 20 REINFORCEMENT WORKSHEET

Colors of the Heart

Complete this worksheet after you finish reading Chapter 20, Section 1.

You will need red and blue colored pencils or crayons for this worksheet.

HELPFUL HINT

The left ventricle and atrium of this heart are on the right side of the page.

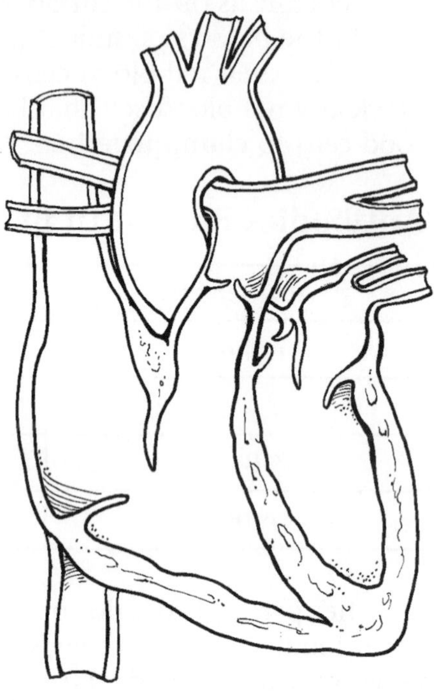

1. The atria are the upper chambers of the heart. The ventricles are the lower chambers of the heart. Label the atria and the ventricles on the diagram.
2. Oxygen-rich blood flows through a vein from the lungs into the left atrium. Color the left atrium and the vein that carries the blood from the lungs red.
3. Blood flows from the left atrium to the left ventricle. Color the left ventricle red.
4. Blood flows through an artery from the left ventricle to the body. The body takes up the oxygen in the blood. Color this artery red.
5. Blood flows through two large veins from the body into the right atrium. Color the right atrium and the two large veins blue.
6. Blood flows from the right atrium to the right ventricle. Color the right ventricle blue.
7. Blood flows through an artery from the right ventricle to the lungs. In the lungs, the blood picks up oxygen. Color this artery blue.
8. Add arrows to your diagram to indicate the flow of blood through the heart. Indicate whether each blood vessel is carrying blood to or from the lungs or the body.

Name ______________________ Date ____________ Class __________

CHAPTER 20 VOCABULARY REVIEW WORKSHEET

A Hunt with Heart

After finishing Chapter 20, give this puzzle a try!

Solve the clues below. Then use the clues to complete the puzzle on the next page.

1. ______________ system that transports materials to and from the body's cells
2. ______________ a connective tissue made up of cells, cell parts, and plasma
3. ______________ the fluid part of blood
4. ______________ largest lymph organ
5. ______________ upper portion of the throat
6. ______________ system that collects extracellular fluid and returns it to your blood
7. ______________ lymph organ just above the heart that produces lymphocytes
8. ______________ fluid and particles absorbed into lymph capillaries
9. ______________ type of blood circulation between the heart and the lungs
10. ______________ the smallest blood vessels in the body
11. ______________ your voice box
12. ______________ expressed in millimeters of Mercury (mm Hg)
13. ______________ cell fragments that clump together to form a plug that helps reduce blood loss
14. ______________ small bean-shaped organs that remove particles from lymph
15. ______________ process that is made up of breathing and cellular respiration
16. ______________ type of blood circulation between the heart and the rest of the body
17. ______________ dome-shaped muscle involved in breathing
18. ______________ upper heart chambers
19. ______________ blood vessels that direct blood away from the heart
20. ______________ made up of groups of lymphatic tissue located inside your throat, at the back of your nasal cavity, and at the back of your tongue

Name ______________________________ Date ______________ Class ______________

21. ______________ this system consists of the lungs, the throat, and the passageways that lead to the lungs

22. ______________ lower heart chambers

23. ______________ blood vessels that direct blood toward the heart

24. ______________ tiny sacs that form the bronchiole branches of the lungs

25. ______________ your windpipe

26. ______________ the two tubes that connect the lungs with the trachea

How many chapter concepts can you find in the block of letters below? Use the clues to help you find them. Words may appear horizontally, vertically, diagonally, or backward.

G	L	Y	M	P	H	A	T	I	C	I	M	E	T	S	Y	S	A
T	I	A	L	V	E	O	L	I	T	O	L	N	M	O	V	L	O
O	B	S	U	R	D	S	H	U	O	C	T	E	F	O	S	Y	S
N	E	L	A	O	E	C	P	A	B	C	A	C	L	Q	Y	M	C
S	H	T	O	I	N	T	H	Y	T	A	P	L	I	M	R	P	A
I	I	L	R	O	X	Y	L	N	D	R	X	N	Y	R	A	H	P
L	B	A	R	O	D	D	T	B	I	D	I	T	R	E	N	N	I
S	Y	B	L	B	I	P	C	Y	G	I	S	A	O	S	O	O	L
E	B	M	A	R	A	L	R	S	U	O	B	O	T	P	M	D	L
L	M	L	P	R	P	A	H	E	E	V	I	X	A	I	L	E	A
C	A	H	G	H	H	T	U	I	S	A	R	L	R	R	U	S	R
I	W	R	O	R	R	E	S	R	P	S	D	T	I	A	P	U	I
R	X	N	Y	R	A	L	E	E	L	C	U	B	P	T	J	M	E
T	C	T	V	S	G	E	Y	T	E	U	P	R	S	I	E	U	S
N	C	A	N	D	M	T	K	R	E	L	I	E	E	O	S	S	R
E	P	E	P	L	A	S	M	A	N	A	Y	M	R	N	T	E	I
V	E	I	N	S	U	M	Y	H	T	R	A	C	H	E	A	Z	N

Name ______________________ Date ____________ Class ____________

CHAPTER 21 REINFORCEMENT WORKSHEET

This System Is Just "Two" Nervous!

Complete this worksheet after you finish reading Chapter 21, Section 1.

Did you know that all the different parts of your body are in constant conversation with one another? Well they are, even though you never hear a word of it! Most of your activities require your **nervous system** to respond to your environment. Read this imaginary conversation between the various parts of your nervous system, and then answer the questions that follow by using the boldface terms as answers.

Brain: Okay everybody, this is Mission Control for the **central** nervous system. It is time to get this body out of bed! Left Arm, would you please shut off the alarm clock already! With that racket, the **Cerebrum** is having trouble remembering what is on the exam in math class today. Left Arm, I am sending signals through **motor neurons** to your muscles now, and I expect you to obey those orders, pronto. Feet, it is time to hit the floor. Signals through your motor neurons are on the way too. This **voluntary movement** will get us to the closet so we can get dressed!

Stomach: Excuse me, but the receptors in my sensory neurons are trying to let you know that the body would like some breakfast. It is awfully empty down here! We also realize that the skin **receptors** are detecting that the room is cold. The sooner we get dressed, the sooner we eat, so hurry!

Brain: I am sorry Stomach, but you will just have to wait. The arms are still involved with other voluntary movement—they are currently combing the hair. By the way, Heart, thank you for pumping all night. You kept us all alive and well. I really have to hand it to the organs on the **involuntary movement** team. This includes you too, Stomach—that late night snack before bed was great, and your digestion process went so smoothly!

Cerebrum: Aha, I've got it! We are having a quiz in math class today, not an exam. Whew, I am so glad I remembered! **Medulla**, I am sorry I didn't remember we needed a coat today. I felt the increase in heart rate you made as we ran back up the stairs. Even though you are only 3 cm long, we couldn't live without you, Medulla.

Spinal Cord: Good morning everyone! All my vertebrae are feeling great today. That new mattress is wonderful. Well, good grief, I have so many impulses from the neurons in the **peripheral** nervous system. The **dendrites** and **axons** of each neuron move information to and from other neurons so quickly. It is amazing I can keep up with you guys!

Peripheral Nervous System: Yes, well, thank you **Spinal Cord**. I have **nerves** throughout the body that I am responsible for, and there is never a moment to waste. I must transfer information to the central nervous system.

Left Hand: Ouch! Pain! Pain! Pain! Spinal Cord, help!

Spinal Cord: Left Hand, stop touching that hot mug!

Cerebellum: Watch out, Legs! Leg Muscles, this is the **Cerebellum**, be quick about it and step to the side, not to the back! You are about to trip over the dog!

Cerebrum: Hey, what just happened? I missed it.

Spinal Cord: Don't worry, Cerebrum, it was just another involuntary movement. The mug we grabbed was too hot to handle, so a reflex prevented the hands from getting burned. I took care of it since you are just too slow, but hey, that's my job.

Questions

1. The nervous system is made up of the ______________________ nervous system and the ______________________ nervous system.

2. The central nervous system is made up of the brain and the ______________________.

3. The peripheral nervous system has many ______________________ throughout the body.

4. Combing your hair, getting out of bed, and getting dressed are all examples of ______________________.

5. The process of digestion and the pumping your heart does are both examples of ______________________.

6. The neurons in your body use ______________________ and ______________________ to transfer information.

7. The ______________________ is responsible for thinking and memory.

8. The ______________________ controls your heart rate, blood pressure, and involuntary breathing.

9. The ______________________ keeps track of the body's position.

10. ______________________ tell your muscles to move.

11. Sensory neurons use ______________________ to tell you when you are hungry and cold.

Name ______________________ Date __________ Class __________

CHAPTER 21

REINFORCEMENT WORKSHEET

The Eyes Have It

Complete this worksheet after you finish reading Chapter 21, Section 2.

Match the descriptions in Column B with the correct structure in Column A, and write the corresponding letter in the appropriate space. When you have finished, use the words in Column A to label the diagram.

Column A	Column B
____ **1.** rods	**a.** holds the photoreceptors
____ **2.** lens	**b.** give a view of the world in grays
____ **3.** optic nerve	**c.** changes pupil size to control the amount of light entering
____ **4.** cones	**d.** focuses light onto the retina
____ **5.** iris	**e.** allows light into the eye
____ **6.** pupil	**f.** interpret bright light; give a colorful view of the world
____ **7.** retina	**g.** takes impulses from the retina to the brain

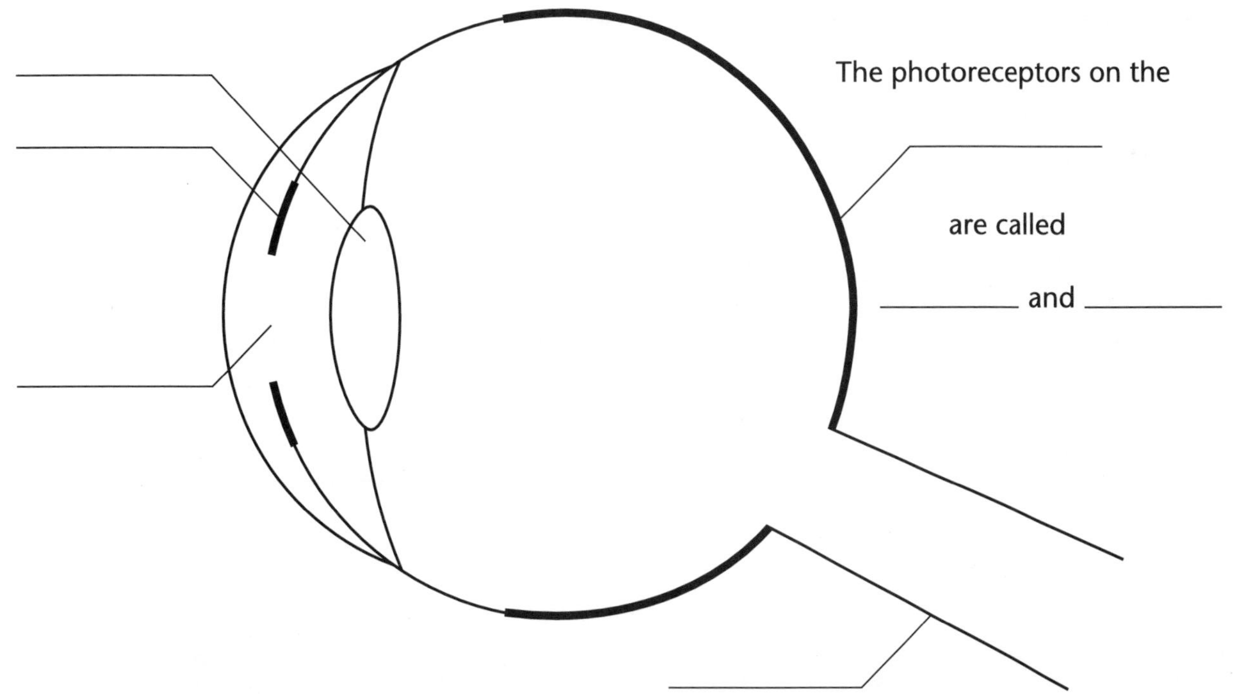

Name ______________________ Date ____________ Class __________

CHAPTER 21 REINFORCEMENT WORKSHEET

Every Gland Lends a Hand

Complete this worksheet after you finish reading Chapter 21, Section 3.

1. How many endocrine glands are discussed in this chapter?

   ____

2. The ______________________ glands regulate the level of calcium in your blood.

3. Which gland controls blood-sugar levels?

   ____

4. When your body responds to stress or danger, it uses the ______________________ glands.

5. Which one of the glands helps your body fight disease?

   ____

6. Your body uses chemical messengers released into the blood, called ______________________, to control body functions.

7. The ______________________ gland increases the rate at which you use energy.

8. Which glands are involved in reproduction?

   ______________________ or ______________________

9. This gland has many functions, one of which is to help the thyroid function properly. Which gland is this?

   ____

10. All these glands are part of the ______________________ system.

11. What are the functions of the endocrine system?

   ____

   ____

   ____

   ____

Name ______________________ Date ____________ Class ____________

CHAPTER 21 **VOCABULARY REVIEW WORKSHEET**

Your Body's Own Language

Give this anagram a try after you finish reading Chapter 21!

1. system in your body responsible for gathering and interpreting information about the body's internal and external environment: URSVNEO

___ ___ ___ ___ ___ ___ ___

2. small snail-shaped organ of the inner ear: CHACOLE

___ ___ ___ ___ ___ ___ ___

3. subdivision of question 1; includes your brain and spinal cord: ANRCELT

___ ___ ___ ___ ___ ___ ___

4. subdivision of your nervous system; collection of nerves: LIPPERHARE

___ ___ ___ ___ ___ ___ ___ ___ ___ ___

5. piece of curved material in the eye that focuses light on the retina: SLEN

___ ___ ___ ___

6. specialized cells that transfer messages as electrical energy: NENORUS

___ ___ ___ ___ ___ ___ ___

7. special neurons in your eye that help you see color: SNOCE

___ ___ ___ ___ ___

8. short branched extensions through which question 6 receives signals: SERENDDIT

___ ___ ___ ___ ___ ___ ___ ___ ___

9. long cell fiber that transmits information to other cells: NOXA

___ ___ ___ ___

10. type of neuron that gathers information about what is happening in and around your body: NYSSREO

___ ___ ___ ___ ___ ___ ___

11. group of cells that makes special chemicals for your body: GNALD

___ ___ ___ ___ ___

12. colored part of the eye: ISRI

___ ___ ___ ___

13. specialized dendrites that detect changes inside or outside the body: OPETCRSER

___ ___ ___ ___ ___ ___ ___ ___ ___

14. send messages from the brain and spinal cord to other systems: OMOTR EOSURNN

__ __ __ __ __   __ __ __ __ __ __ __

15. axons that are bundled together with blood vessels and connective tissue: NSREVE

__ __ __ __ __ __

16. the largest organ of the central nervous system: ARNIB

__ __ __ __ __

17. chemical messengers produced by the endocrine glands: SHORNMOE

__ __ __ __ __ __ __ __

18. part of question 16 where thinking takes place: CREUMBER

__ __ __ __ __ __ __ __

19. part of question 16 that helps you keep your balance: MULERBECLE

__ __ __ __ __ __ __ __ __ __

20. transfers electrical impulses from the eye to the brain: COPTI VERNE

__ __ __ __ __   __ __ __ __ __

21. part of question 16 that connects to the spinal cord: DELUALM

__ __ __ __ __ __ __

22. a quick, involuntary action: FELEXR

__ __ __ __ __ __

23. system that controls body functions such as sexual development: CODENINER

__ __ __ __ __ __ __ __ __

24. the light-sensitive layer of cells at the back of the eye: ETNRAI

__ __ __ __ __ __

25. special neurons in the eye that detect light: EPSERROOPTHTCO

__ __ __ __ __ __ __ __ __ __ __ __ __ __

26. electrical messages that pass along the neurons: SPULIMES

__ __ __ __ __ __ __ __

27. type of question 25 that can detect very dim light: DSRO

__ __ __ __

Name ______________________ Date ____________ Class ____________

CHAPTER 22 REINFORCEMENT WORKSHEET

Reproduction Review

Complete this worksheet after you finish reading Chapter 22, Section 1.

Different organisms reproduce in different ways. Fill in the table below by circling the correct type of reproduction. Then indicate the organism's method of fertilization and where the embryo develops. Several boxes have been filled in to get you started.

Organism	Type of reproduction	Method of fertilization	Where the embryo develops
Hydra	asexual or sexual		none (no embryo)
Whale	asexual or sexual		
Chicken	asexual or sexual		
Frog	asexual or sexual		
Sea star	asexual or sexual	none	
Echidna	asexual or sexual		
Fish	asexual or sexual		
Human	asexual or sexual		inside the mother (placental)
Kangaroo	asexual or sexual		

Name ______________________ Date ____________ Class ____________

CHAPTER 22 REINFORCEMENT WORKSHEET

The Beginning of a Life

Complete this worksheet after you have finished reading Chapter 22, Section 3.

The following illustration shows the development of a human. Choose the term from the list below left that best labels what is indicated in the diagram, and write the term in the corresponding box. Then, match each feature below right to the stage where it develops, and write the corresponding letter in the blank. Each feature and term is used once. Stages may have more than one feature.

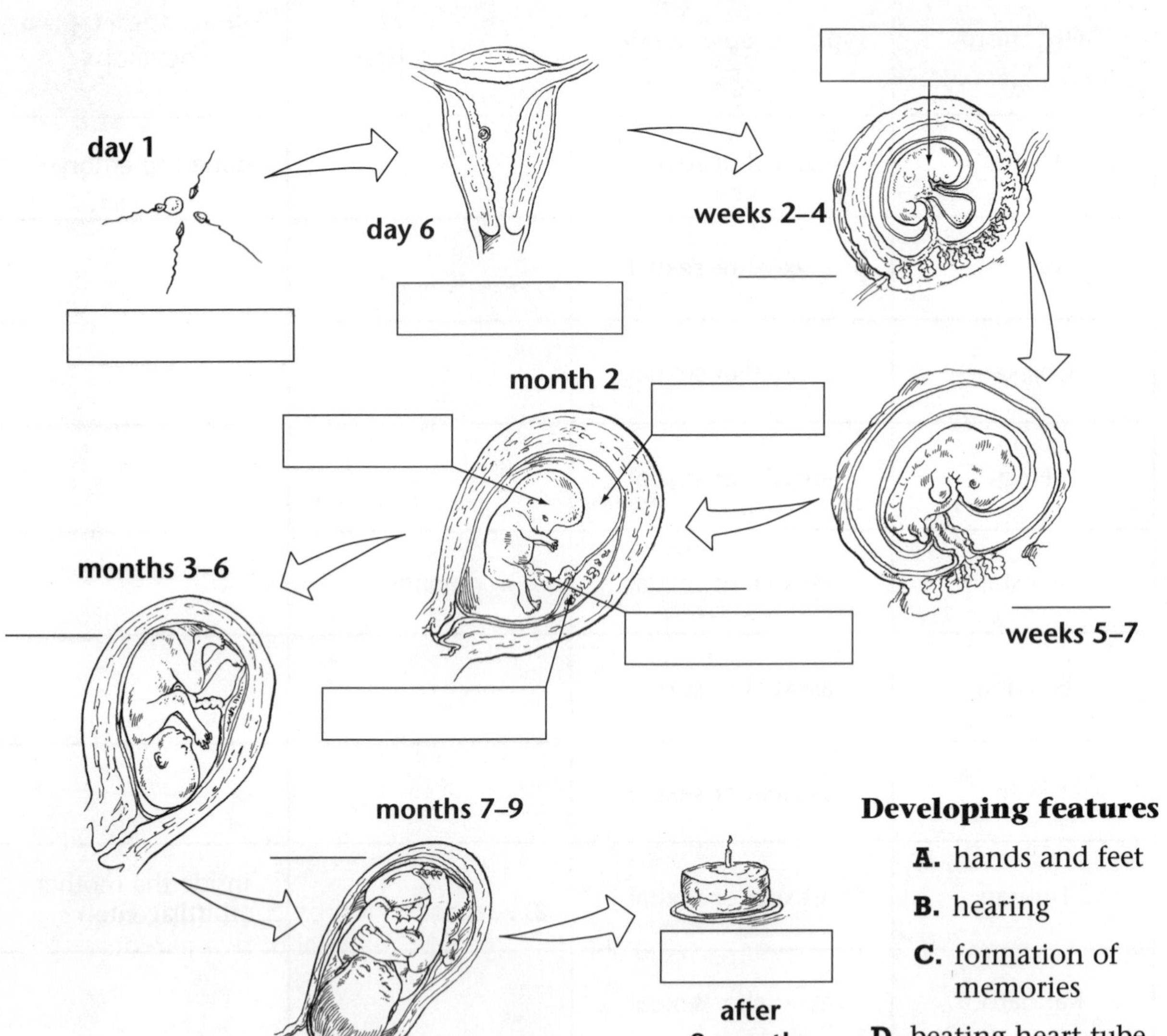

Developing features

A. hands and feet
B. hearing
C. formation of memories
D. beating heart tube
E. muscle movement
F. blinking and swallowing
G. taste buds and eyebrows
H. lungs "practice breathing"
I. limb buds and facial features
J. beginning of brain and spinal cord

Terms

umbilical cord	fetus
birth	implantation
fertilization	placenta
amnion	embryo

Name ______________________ Date ____________ Class __________

CHAPTER 22 VOCABULARY REVIEW WORKSHEET

A Reproduction Crossword

Complete this puzzle after you finish Chapter 22.

ACROSS

2. sexually ________ diseases pass from an infected to an uninfected person during sexual contact

4. an embryo after 8 weeks of development

7. special two-way exchange organ that provides nutrients and oxygen to the fetus and removes its wastes

9. gives birth to partially-developed live young

10. an example of a monotreme

12. connects the embryo and the placenta

16. organ where the fetus develops

17. tube inside the penis that carries semen to the outside of the body

18. organism that reproduces through budding

20. organ that makes sperm and testosterone

22. a mixture of sperm and fluids

25. a cell created from the combined nuclei of the egg and sperm

DOWN

1. a tube where sperm mix with fluids from glands

3. monthly discharge of blood and uterine lining

4. tube that leads from an ovary to the uterus

5. unable to have children

6. passageway for a baby from the uterus to the outside of the body

8. when a broken-off part of the parent's body develops into an offspring

10. temporary storage place for male sex cells

11. the time of life when sex organs mature

13. when a developed egg is released into the fallopian tubes

14. a skin-covered sac where the testes rest

15. female organs where eggs are produced

19. reproductive organ that transfers semen into the female's body during sexual intercourse

21. reproduction by combining the genetic material of two parents

23. ball of cells that must embed itself in the uterus to survive

24. produced in the seminiferous tubules

A Reproduction Crossword, continued

Answer Key

Reinforcement & Vocabulary Review Worksheets

▪ CONTENTS ▪

Name ______________ Date ______________ Class ______________

CHAPTER 1 REINFORCEMENT WORKSHEET

The Mystery of the Bubbling Top

Complete this worksheet after you have finished reading Chapter 1, Section 2. Use the materials at right to conduct the activity below. Then answer the questions that follow.

MATERIALS
- small, empty plastic soda bottle
- cold water
- plastic or plastic-foam disposable plate
- scissors
- hot water
- beaker or other container large enough to hold the soda bottle

1. Fill the empty bottle halfway with cold water.
2. Cut a quarter-sized disk from the plastic plate.
3. Moisten the plastic disk, and place it on top of the bottle's neck.
4. Pour hot water into the beaker until it is about one-quarter full.
5. Carefully place the bottle inside the beaker.
6. What happened to the plastic disk?

   Sample answer: The plastic disk began to move on top of the bottle's neck.

You just made observations.

7. Why do you think the plastic disk did that? Brainstorm for as many answers as possible. Then put a star next to the explanation you consider most reasonable.

   Accept all reasonable responses. Sample starred answer: I think the plastic disk moved because the hot water warmed the air inside the bottle.

You just formed a hypothesis.

8. How could you test your hypothesis? Outline an experiment you could conduct.

   Sample answer: I could try placing the bottle in a beaker of cold water to see if the plastic disk moves.

Name ______________________ Date ____________ Class __________

The Mystery of the Bubbling Top, continued

9. Conduct your experiment. What happens?

Sample answer: The disk does not move.

You just tested your hypothesis.

10. How do you explain the results of your experiment?

Sample answer: I think that the disk does not move because the cold water cannot heat up the air inside the bottle.

You just analyzed the results of your experiment.

11. Do the results of your experiment match your hypothesis? Explain.

Sample answer: Yes; if the disk had started moving as soon as it did before, I would have known that the temperature of the water had nothing to do with the movement of the disk.

12. Do you need to conduct more experiments to find out if your hypothesis is correct? Why or why not?

Sample answer: Yes; there are more factors that I could change. Next, I could try changing the temperature of the water inside the bottle to see what happens.

You just drew conclusions.

Congratulations!
You have just finished the first steps of the scientific method! Share your results with your classmates.

Name ______________________ Date ____________ Class __________

The Puzzling World of Life Science, continued

1. T E C H N O L O G Y
2. T H E O R Y
3. A R E A
4. W A T E R
5. V O L U M E
6. X R A Y S
7. C O N T R O L L E D E X P E R I M E N T
8. P R E D I C T I O N
9. C O M P O U N D L I G H T
10. L I F E S C I E N C E
11. C O N C L U S I O N S
12. V A R I A B L E
13. S C I E N T I F I C M E T H O D
14. T E M P E R A T U R E
15. M A S S
16. F A C T O R
17. M R I
18. H Y P O T H E S I S
19. E L E C T R O N M I C R O S C O P E
20. C O M M U N I C A T E
21. M E T E R

Name ______________ Date ______ Class ______

CHAPTER 2 REINFORCEMENT WORKSHEET

Amazing Discovery

Complete this worksheet after you finish reading Chapter 2, Section 2.

Imagine that you are a biologist on a mission to Mars. You have just discovered what you think is a simple single-celled Martian organism. For now, you are calling it Alpha. Before you can claim that you have discovered life on Mars, however, you need to show that Alpha is alive.

1. What are the six characteristics you will look for to see if Alpha is alive?

a. Does it have cells?

b. Does it respond to change?

c. Does it reproduce?

d. Does it have DNA?

e. Does it use energy?

f. Does it grow and develop?

2. Outline a test or experiment to verify one of the characteristics you listed above.

Accept any reasonable answer. Sample answer: To see if Alpha responds to change, I will present it with different stimuli, such as bright lights and chemicals, to see if it reacts. If it does, the results will help show that Alpha is alive. If it doesn't, I'll know that it is not alive.

3. If you can show that Alpha is alive, you will take it back to Earth for further study. What will you need to provide Alpha with to keep it alive?

I'll need to provide Alpha with the necessities of life: food (or an energy source so Alpha can make its own food), water, air, and a place to live.

Name ______________ Date ______ Class ______

CHAPTER 2 REINFORCEMENT WORKSHEET

Building Blocks

Complete this worksheet after you finish reading Chapter 2, Section 3.

Each of the boxes below represents one of the five compounds that are found in all cells. The phrases at the bottom of the page describe these compounds. Match each of the descriptions to the appropriate compound. Then write the corresponding letter in the appropriate box. Some descriptions may be used more than once.

Compounds in Cells

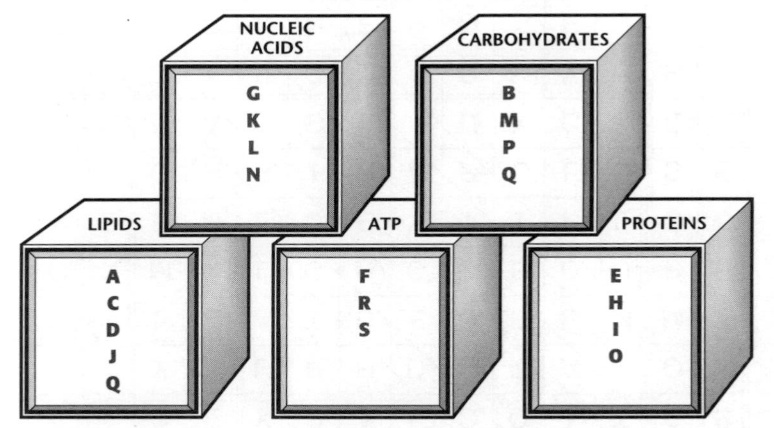

Clues

A. fat in animals
B. made of sugars
C. oil in plants
D. one type forms much of the cell membrane
E. enzymes
F. major fuel used for the cell's activities
G. "blueprints" of life
H. subunits are amino acids
I. hemoglobin
J. cannot mix with water
K. DNA
L. tells the cell how to make proteins
M. can be simple or complex
N. subunits called nucleotides
O. make up spider webs and hair
P. starch in plants
Q. source of stored energy
R. adenosine triphosphate
S. energy in lipids and carbohydrates is transferred to this molecule

Name ________________ Date ________ Class ________

CHAPTER 2 **VOCABULARY REVIEW WORKSHEET**

It's Alive!

Complete this puzzle after you finish Chapter 2.

In the space provided, write the term described by the clue. Then find these words in the puzzle. Terms can be hidden in the puzzle vertically, horizontally, diagonally or backwards.

1. stimulus — change in an organism's environment that affects the activity of an organism
2. carbohydrates — group of compounds made of sugars
3. homeostasis — maintenance of a stable internal environment
4. starch — complex carbohydrate made by plants
5. heredity — transmission of characteristics from one generation to the next
6. metabolism — chemical activities of an organism necessary for life
7. nucleic acid — made up of subunits called nucleotides
8. consumer — eats other organisms for food
9. decomposer — organism that breaks down the nutrients of dead organisms or wastes for food
10. phospholipids — two layers of these form much of the cell membrane
11. enzymes — proteins that speed up certain chemical reactions
12. DNA — molecule that provides instructions for making proteins
13. producer — organism that can produce its own food
14. cell — membrane-covered structure that contains all materials necessary for life
15. asexual — reproduction in which a single parent produces offspring that are identical to the parent
16. lipid — chemical compound that cannot mix with water and that is used to store energy
17. protein — large molecule made up of amino acids
18. ATP — energy in food is transferred to this molecule
19. sexual — reproduction in which two parents are necessary to produce offspring that share characteristics of both parents

Name ________________ Date ________ Class ________

It's Alive! continued

D	P	H	O	S	P	H	O	L	I	P	I	D	S
N	S	D	T	E	R	P	U	I	R	C	S	E	I
A	A	S	E	X	U	A	L	O	O	I	T	C	S
R	C	Y	Z	U	P	H	D	S	T	A	I	O	A
C	E	L	L	A	T	U	E	D	R	B	M	M	T
O	N	M	X	L	C	H	C	D	E	D	U	P	S
N	Z	E	H	E	C	E	Y	I	I	P	L	O	O
S	Y	O	R	R	I	H	A	P	L	L	U	S	E
U	M	N	A	R	O	L	I	U	X	C	S	E	M
M	E	T	A	B	O	L	I	S	M	Y	U	R	O
E	S	E	R	L	N	P	R	O	T	E	I	N	H
R	H	A	M	Z	Y	T	I	D	E	R	E	H	E
A	C	E	D	I	C	A	C	I	E	L	C	U	N

Name ______________ Date ________ Class ________

CHAPTER 3 REINFORCEMENT WORKSHEET

Light Interactions

Complete this worksheet after you finish reading Chapter 3, Section 2.

Your good friend, Roy G. Biv, has written out a list of the ways light waves interact. Roy knows a lot about light waves, but he doesn't know the scientific terms. Help Roy arrange his notes so that every definition or example on his list is in the appropriate box below. Some notes may be used more than once.

Reflection	Absorption	Scattering
occurs when a light wave bounces off an object causes cats' eyes to glow at night allows you to see yourself in a mirror why you detect green light coming from a lime	occurs when energy from light waves is transferred to particles in matter causes a flashlight beam to become dimmer the farther away from the flashlight it travels why a window glass feels warm on a sunny day why you do not detect red light coming from a lime	occurs when light energy is released from particles that have extra energy allows you to see objects outside the beam of light causes the sky to appear blue affects light with short wavelengths more than light with long wavelengths causes a flashlight beam to become dimmer the farther away from the flashlight it travels

Roy's Notes on Light

- causes a flashlight beam to become dimmer the farther away from the flashlight it travels
- why a window glass feels warm on a sunny day
- why you detect green light coming from a lime
- why you do not detect red light coming from a lime
- occurs when light energy is released from particles that have extra energy
- allows you to see yourself in a mirror
- occurs when energy from light waves is transferred to particles in matter
- causes the sky to appear blue
- allows you to see objects outside the beam of light
- causes cats' eyes to glow at night
- affects light with short wavelengths more than light with long wavelengths
- occurs when a light wave bounces off an object

Name ______________ Date ________ Class ________

CHAPTER 3 VOCABULARY REVIEW WORKSHEET

A Light Puzzle

Try this anagram after you finish Chapter 3.

Use the definitions below to unscramble the vocabulary words.

1. the passing of light through matter — SATRINMISSON — transmission
2. the transfer of energy carried by light waves to particles in matter — TIPABNOROS — absorption
3. the number of waves produced in a given amount of time — QUECENFRY — frequency
4. a lens that is thinner in the middle than at the edges — ONACCEV — concave
5. the release of light energy by particles of matter that have absorbed extra energy — GICANSTERT — scattering
6. the bouncing back of a wave after it strikes a barrier or object — LEFTECRONI — reflection
7. a curved, transparent object that forms an image by refracting light — SLEN — lens
8. the distance between one point on a wave and the corresponding point on the next wave — VATHELWENG — wavelength
9. waves that do not require a medium — TICELOCATREMNEG — electromagnetic
10. a lens that is thicker in the middle than at the edges — NEXVOC — convex
11. disturbance that transmits energy through matter or space — VEAW — wave
12. material that gives a substance its color by reflecting some colors of light and absorbing others — PNETGIM — pigment
13. the bending of a wave as it passes at an angle from one medium to another — CRATERFONI — refraction

Name ______________________ Date ____________ Class ____________

CHAPTER 4 REINFORCEMENT WORKSHEET

An Ecosystem

Complete this worksheet after you finish reading Chapter 4, Section 1. Examine the picture below. It shows living and nonliving things existing in an ecosystem. Fill in the table to describe the organization of this ecosystem.

Sample answer:

Nonliving things	Populations
air	deer
river	trees
rocks	grass
rain	flowers
	butterflies

1. What makes up the community in this ecosystem?

A community is made up of the populations of living things in the ecosystem. So the community in this ecosystem is the deer, trees, grass, flowers, and butterflies.

Name ______________________ Date ____________ Class ____________

CHAPTER 4 REINFORCEMENT WORKSHEET

Building a Eukaryotic Cell

Complete this worksheet after you finish reading Chapter 4, Section 3. Below is a list of the features found in eukaryotic cells. Next to each feature, write a *P* if it is a feature found only in plant cells and a *B* if it is a feature that can be found in both plant and animal cells.

1. B endoplasmic reticulum
2. B mitochondria
3. B nucleus
4. P vacuole
5. B cell membrane
6. B cytoplasm
7. B ribosomes
8. B Golgi complex
9. P cell wall
10. B vesicles
11. B DNA
12. B nucleolus
13. P chloroplasts

In the space provided, label the structures of the eukaryotic cell drawn below. Include all of the structures that you labeled *B*.

A Eukaryotic Cell

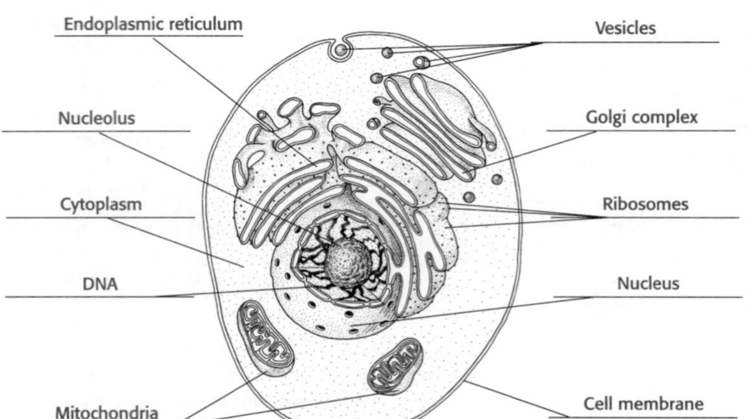

Name ______________________ Date __________ Class __________

A Cell Crossword Puzzle, continued

1 CYTOPLASM
1 COMMUNITY
2 CELL WALL
3 RIBOSOMES
4 DNA
5 TISSUE
6 BACTERIA
7 EUKARYOTIC
8 VESICLES
9 NUCLEUS
10 POPULATION
11 LYSOSOME
12 PROKARYOTIC
13 MITOCHONDRIA
14 GOLGI COMPLEX
15 CELL MEMBRANE
16 NUCLEOLUS
17 CELL THEORY
18 MULTICELLULAR
19 ER
20 ATP
21 ECOSYSTEM
22 CELL
23 ORGAN
24 VACUOLE
25 HOOKE
26 CHLOROPLAST
27 ORGANISM
28 ORGAN SYSTEMS
29 ORGANELLE

Name ______________________ Date __________ Class __________

CHAPTER 5 REINFORCEMENT WORKSHEET

Into and Out of the Cell

Complete this worksheet after you have finished reading Chapter 5, Section 1.

Each of the boxes below represents a different method cells use to bring small particles into the cell or to take small particles out of the cell. Add the notes at the bottom of the page to the appropriate box. Be careful—some notes can be used more than once.

Small Particle Transport

Osmosis	Passive Transport	Active Transport
particles move through cell membrane between phospholipid molecules particles move from an area of high concentration to an area of low concentration water does not require ATP	particles move through protein doorways particles move from an area of high concentration to an area of low concentration sugar or amino acids does not require ATP	particles move through protein doorways particles move from an area of low concentration to an area of high concentration requires ATP

Notes

- particles move through protein doorways
- particles move through cell membrane between phospholipid molecules
- sugar or amino acids
- requires ATP
- particles move from an area of high concentration to an area of low concentration
- does not require ATP
- particles move from an area of low concentration to an area of high concentration
- water

Name ______________ Date ________ Class ________

CHAPTER 5 REINFORCEMENT WORKSHEET

Activities of the Cell

Complete this worksheet after you have finished reading Chapter 5, Section 2.

1. Sketch and label a chloroplast and a mitochondrion in the space provided.

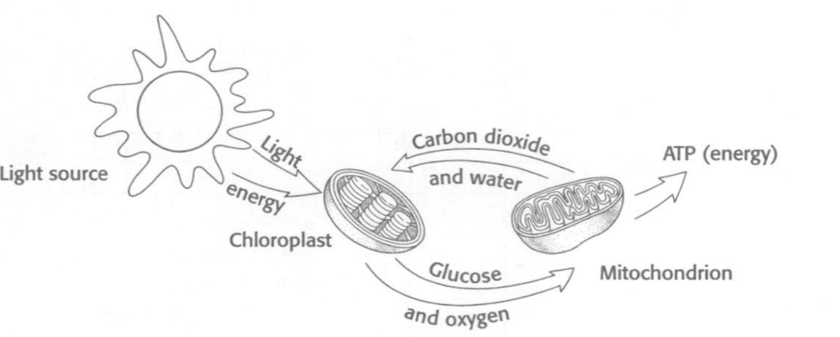

2. Chloroplasts use light energy during photosynthesis. To your drawing add a light source and an arrow from the light source to the chloroplast.
3. Chloroplasts give off oxygen and glucose during photosynthesis. Mitochondria use oxygen and glucose during cellular respiration. Add this information to your diagram.
4. During cellular respiration, mitochondria produce ATP. Add this information to your diagram.
5. Besides light energy, what do chloroplasts use to make glucose?

   Chloroplasts also need carbon dioxide and water to make glucose.

6. Besides ATP, what do mitochondria give off during cellular respiration?

   Mitochondria also give off carbon dioxide, water, and energy during cellular respiration.

7. Add the information from questions 5 and 6 to your diagram.

Name ______________ Date ________ Class ________

CHAPTER 5 REINFORCEMENT WORKSHEET

This is Radio KCEL

Complete this worksheet after you have finished reading Chapter 5, Section 3.

Hello, Cell-O-Rama radio fans! Katy Chromosome here. We have a very exciting program in store for you: *Cell Mitosis in Action,* with local sports announcers Sid Toekinesis and Dee Ennay. To make this a Cell-O-Rama challenge, we've spliced the sound clips from each phase of mitosis in the wrong order. Your job is to identify the correct phase for each clip and then put the clips in the correct sequence. Good luck! Dee and Sid?

Sid: Thanks, Katy. Let's roll the tape, Dee.

Dee: Rolling . . .

Segment A: Mitosis Phase 3

Sid: Dee, I think the Chromatid twins are really mad this time. They seem to be storming off in opposite directions. Don't they care about the game?

Dee: This is just incredible, Sid. Wait a minute! Both groups appear to be moving into huddles. Is the game over? Do you think they'll come back?

Segment B: Mitosis Phase 1

Sid: Dee, this is UN-believable. The Chromatid twins are shrinking! Are they getting ready for a fight?

Dee: Sid, I am brand new to this game, and I just don't know what might happen next. Where on *Earth* are those centrioles going?

Sid: Dee, I think things are getting too hot for them. They are hightailing it out of there.

Dee: Oh no. They seem to be throwing a net to trap the Chromatid twins. It looks like the centrioles are herding them to the center of the field.

Segment C: Mitosis Phase 4

Sid: This is truly amazing, Dee. Some sort of barrier seems to be forming around each of the huddles. What is going on?

Dee: Sid, believe it or not, I think the teams are taking a timeout. See how they're all unwinding? They have worked hard today. This has been *quite* a game!

Segment D: Mitosis Phase 2

Sid: Dee, maybe they're getting ready for a kickoff. The twins are lining up along the center of the field. I think they're waiting for a signal.

Dee: Sid, you can just *feel* the tension in the air. Uh oh. I think a fight just broke out. Wait—they're all *wrestling* out there! The twins look like they're trying to get away from each other. Where are the refs when you need them?

Name ______________ Date ________ Class ________

CHAPTER 5 VOCABULARY REVIEW WORKSHEET

Cell Game Show

After you finish Chapter 5, give this puzzle a try!

This game may be played individually or in teams. You are supplied with the answers to questions in four categories. Your challenge is to come up with the correct question for each answer. Each correct "question" has a point value corresponding to the number at the beginning of the row. Keep a running total of your points as you play.

	To Make Two	On the Move	Lazy Days	I Can "C" You
50	These condense into an X-shape before mitosis. What are chromatids?	How a cell membrane moves large particles into the cell. What is endocytosis?	The movement of particles from an area of high concentration to an area of low concentration. What is diffusion?	This process ends when a cell divides and new cells are formed. What is the cell cycle?
100	Human body cells have 23 pairs of these. What are homologous chromosomes?	The movement of particles through proteins against the normal direction of diffusion. What is active transport?	Oxygen can slip between these molecules, which make up much of the cell membrane. What are phospholipids?	This is the region where chromatids are held together. What is a centromere?
200	Bacteria double this way. What is binary fission?	This word means "outside the cell." What is exocytosis?	Diffusion of water across a membrane. What is osmosis?	The way organisms get energy from food using oxygen. What is cellular respiration?
500	The complicated process of chromosome separation; the second stage of the cell cycle. What is mitosis?	The process by which plants capture light energy and change it into food. What is photosynthesis?	The diffusion of particles through special "doorways" in the cell membrane. What is passive transport?	The cytoplasm splits in two during this process. What is cytokinesis?
1000	During the third stage of the cell cycle, this forms in eukaryotic cells with cell walls. What is a cell plate?	When there's no oxygen for your cells, they use this to get energy. What is fermentation?	Special doorways in the cell membrane are made of these. What are proteins?	Oxygen can pass directly through this cell part. What is the cell membrane?

Total Points: ________

Name ______________ Date ________ Class ________

CHAPTER 6 REINFORCEMENT WORKSHEET

Dimples and DNA

Complete this worksheet after you have finished reading Chapter 6, Section 1.

In humans, dimpled cheeks are a dominant trait, with a genotype of ***DD*** or ***Dd***. Nondimpled cheeks are a recessive trait, with a genotype of ***dd***.

1. Imagine that Parent A, with the genotype ***DD***, has dimpled cheeks. Parent B has the genotype ***dd*** and does not have dimpled cheeks.

The Punnett square below diagrams the cross between Parent A and Parent B. Complete the Punnett square. (The first square has been done for you. You may want to refer to How to Make a Punnett square in your text.)

Parent A

Parent B	D	D
d	Dd	Dd
d	Dd	Dd

2. A Punnett square shows what genotypes are possible for the offspring of a certain cross. What genotypes are possible for the offspring of Parent A and Parent B?

Only the genotype Dd is possible for the offspring of Parent A and Parent B.

3. Each of the four squares of a Punnett square represents a 25 percent probability that the offspring will have that particular genotype. What is the probability that the offspring of Parent A and Parent B will have dimpled cheeks?

The probability that the offspring of Parent A and Parent B will have dimpled cheeks is 25% + 25% + 25% + 25% = 100%.

Name ______________________ Date __________ Class __________

Dimples and DNA, continued

4. Parent X, with the genotype ***Dd,*** has dimpled cheeks. Parent Y also has the genotype ***Dd*** and has dimpled cheeks as well. To find out what their offspring might look like, complete the Punnett square below.

Parent X

Parent Y	D	d
D	DD	Dd
d	Dd	dd

5. What is the probability that the offspring of Parent X and Parent Y will have each of the following genotypes?

DD: 25%

Dd: 25% + 25% = 50%

dd: 25%

6. What is the probability that the offspring of Parent X and Parent Y will have nondimpled cheeks?

The probability of these offspring having nondimpled cheeks is 25 percent.

7. What is the probability that the offspring of Parent X and Parent Y will have dimpled cheeks? (Remember that there are two genotypes that can produce dimpled cheeks.)

The probability of these offspring having dimpled cheeks is 75 percent.

Name ______________________ Date __________ Class __________

Vocabulary Garden, continued

1. H O M O L O **G** O U S
2. S E X C H **R** O M O S O M E S
3. A L L **E** L E S
4. **G** E N O T Y P E
5. M I T **O** S I S
6. H E **R** E D I T Y
7. **M** E I O S I S
8. R E C **E** S S I V E
9. P U N **N** E T T S Q U A R E
10. **D** O M I N A N T
11. B R **E** E D I N G
12. P O **L** L I N A T I N G
13. **S** P E R M
14. P H E N O T Y **P** E
15. **E** G G S
16. P R O B **A** B I L I T Y
17. G E N E **S**

18. What do Gregor Mendel's peas have to do with the study of heredity?

Sample answer: Mendel used pea plants to study how traits are passed from parents to offspring. Mendel's results showed that each plant got two sets of instructions for each characteristic—one set from each parent plant.

Name ______________ Date ______ Class ______

CHAPTER 7 REINFORCEMENT WORKSHEET

DNA Mutations

Complete this worksheet after reading Chapter 7, Section 2.

DNA is made up of nucleotides that each contain a sugar, a phosphate, and a base. The four possible bases are: adenine, cytosine, thymine, and guanine. Remember that adenine and thymine are complementary and form pairs, and cytosine and guanine are complementary and form pairs.

1. Below is half of a section of DNA that has been split apart and is ready to copy itself. Write the appropriate letter in the space provided to build the DNA's new complementary strand.

G - - - - - - - - - - C
T - - - - - - - - - - A
A - - - - - - - - - - T
A - - - - - - - - - - T
C - - - - - - - - - - G
T - - - - - - - - - - A
C - - - - - - - - - - G
C - - - - - - - - - - G
T - - - - - - - - - - A

2. Sometimes mistakes happen when the DNA is being copied. These mistakes, or mutations, change the order of the bases in DNA. There are three kinds of mutations that can occur in DNA: deletion, insertion, and substitution.

a. Below are two sequences—an original sequence of bases in DNA and the sequence of bases after a mutation has occurred. On the original base sequence, show where the mutation has occurred by circling the appropriate base pair, and write what type of mutation it is in the space provided.

Base sequence in original cell DNA	Base sequence in a cell with mutated DNA
C G	C G
T A	T A
C G	C G
C G	C G
T A	T A
A T	A T
A T	A T
A T	A T
(C G)	T A
C G	C G
T A	T A

substitution

Name ______________ Date ______ Class ______

b. Below are two more sequences—an original sequence of bases in DNA and the sequence of bases after a mutation has occurred. On the original base sequence, show where the mutation has occurred by circling the appropriate base pair, and write what type of mutation it is in the space provided.

Base sequence in original cell DNA	Base sequence in a cell with mutated DNA
C G	C G
T A	T A
A T	A T
C G	C G
C G	C G
G C	G C
T A	T A
A T	A T
A T	A T
(G C)	A T
A T	T A
T A	

deletion

3. Ribosomes "read" a complementary copy of DNA in order to make proteins. Each group of three bases forms the code for an amino acid. When mutations occur in DNA, they can change the information that the DNA carries.

To understand this process better, look at the sentence below, which uses only three-letter words.

AMY GOT THE RED HOT POT OFF THE LOG

If one letter is deleted from this sentence, it becomes:

AMY GTT HER EDH OTP OTO FFT HEL OG

How is this similar to what can happen when a mutation occurs in DNA?

When a mutation occurs in DNA, the DNA might no longer carry the same information.

Name ______________ Date ________ Class ________

CHAPTER 7 VOCABULARY REVIEW WORKSHEET

Unraveling Genes

Try this puzzle after you finish reading Chapter 7!
Solve the clues and unscramble the letters to fill in the blanks. Fill the letters in the squares and read the final clue to unravel the secret message.

1. Molecule that carries our hereditary information: NAD
D(11) N A

2. Subunits of DNA: DISTONEUCLE
N U C L E O T I(1) D E S

3. Nucleotide base known as A: ENIDANE
A(16) D E N I(14) N E

4. Complement of question 3: TIEHYMN
T H Y M(5) I N E

5. Nucleotide base known as G: NUANIGE
G U A N I N(15) E

6. Complement of question 5: YOSTINCE
C Y T O(4) S I N E

7. Shape of a DNA molecule (two words): EXELLIDOBUH
D O(12) U B L E H E L(7) I X

8. Organelle that manufactures proteins: MOOSERIB
R I B O S O M E(10)

9. A change in the order of the bases of an organism's DNA: UNMATIOT
M(13) U T A T I O N(17)

10. Anything that can cause damage to DNA: UNGATEM
M U T(9) A G E N

11. A tool for tracing a trait through generations of a family: DEEPGIRE
P(6) E D I G R E E

12. Manipulation of genes that allows scientists to put genes from one organism into another organism: (two words) NEETIEGGINGECINNER
G E N E T I C(18)
E N G I N E E R I N G

Name ______________ Date ________ Class ________

Unraveling Genes, continued

13. Analysis of fragments of DNA as a form of identification (two words): PANDINGINGFRENRIT
D N A F I N G E(19) R P R I N T I N G

14. Genes are located on these structures that are found in the nucleus of most cells: SHROCOMEMOS
C H R O M O S O M E(8) S

15. DNA that results when genes from one organism are put into another organism using genetic engineering: BINRANTECOM
R E C(3) O M B I N A N T

16. The goal of the Human ________ Project is to map the location and sequence of all our genes: MONEEG
G E N(2) O M E

FINAL CLUE:

Occurs when different traits are equally dominant and each allele has its own degree of influence:

I	N	C	O	M	P	L	E	T	E
1	2	3	4	5	6	7	8	9	10

D	O	M	I	N	A	N	C	E
11	12	13	14	15	16	17	18	19

Name ______________________ Date __________ Class __________

CHAPTER 8 REINFORCEMENT WORKSHEET

Bicentennial Celebration

Complete this worksheet after reading Chapter 8, Section 2.

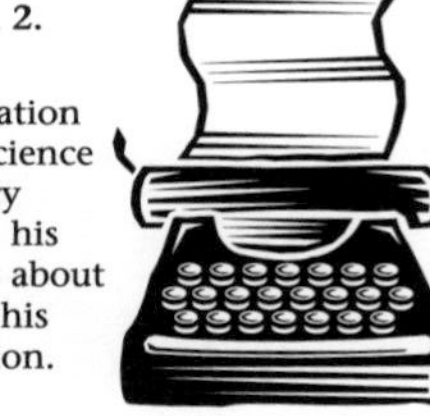

Imagine that it is 2059—the 200th anniversary of the publication of Darwin's *On the Origin of Species*. You are a reporter for a science magazine that is publishing a special issue about evolutionary biology. Your assignment is to write an article about Darwin, his travels, and his scientific theory of evolution. Include details about the Galápagos finches and how Darwin first got the idea for his theory, and explain the steps in the process of natural selection. Don't forget to give your article an eye-catching headline!

Accept any reasonable answer. Sample answer:

The Mysterious Galápagos Finches

In 1831, Charles Darwin, a natural scientist, traveled around the world on the HMS *Beagle*. On the Galápagos Islands, 965 km off the coast of Equador, Darwin discovered his mysterious finches. The Galápagos finches are similar to those found in South America, but they are distinguished by the shape of their beaks and the food they eat. Darwin theorized that the finches originally came from the mainland but, over many generations, adapted to the different ways the finches obtain food in the environment of the Galápagos Islands. Darwin thought that populations of organisms change slowly over time by a process called natural selection. The four steps in natural selection are overproduction, genetic variation, the struggle to survive, and successful reproduction. During overproduction, organisms produce more offspring than can survive. Some of the offspring have different traits from each other, and this is genetic variation. During the struggle to survive, organisms with certain traits are more likely to survive. The organisms that survive pass on those traits to their young through successful reproduction. Over many generations, the process of natural selection can create new species.

Name ______________________ Date __________ Class __________

CHAPTER 8 VOCABULARY REVIEW WORKSHEET

Charles Darwin's Legacy

After you finish Chapter 8, give this puzzle a try.
Unscramble each of the words below, and write the word in the space provided.

1. SISEPCE	a group of organisms that can mate to produce fertile offspring	S P E C I (E) S
2. CATEISPOIN	the process by which two populations become so different they can no longer interbreed	S P E C I A T (I) O N
3. ASTRIT	distinguishing qualities that can be passed on from parents to offspring	T R A I (T) S
4. SVELETICE	________ breeding is the breeding of organisms that have a certain desired trait.	S E L E C T I (V) E
5. TAPATIDONA	a hereditary characteristic that helps an organism survive and reproduce in its environment	A D A P T A T I (O) N
6. ALTRAUN	Successful reproduction is the fourth step of ________ selection.	(N) A T U R A L
7. GLEVITIAS	describes once-useful structures	V E S T I G I A (L)
8. SLOSFIS	solidified remains of once-living organisms	F (O) S S I L S
9. MAUTONTI	a change in a gene at the DNA level	M (U) T A T I O N

Now unscramble the circled letters to find Darwin's legacy.

E V O L U T I O N

Name ______________________ Date ____________ Class ____________

CHAPTER 9 REINFORCEMENT WORKSHEET

Earth Timeline

Complete this worksheet after you finish reading Chapter 9, Section 1.
Scientists use four major divisions to talk about the Earth's history: Precambrian time, the Paleozoic era, the Mesozoic era, and the Cenozoic era. Precambrian time lasted for about 88 percent of the 4.6 billion years of Earth's history. The Paleozoic era was about 6.3 percent of Earth's history. The Mesozoic era was about 4.0 percent of Earth's history. The Cenozoic era has lasted for about 1.4 percent of the Earth's history.

The Earth's history is difficult to imagine because it is so long. But what if the entire history of the Earth could fit into a single human life span of 80 years? Fill in the timeline below to show how old a person would be when each era begins. If the first single-celled organism appeared 3.5 billion years ago, how old would the person be when the first single-celled organism appears on Earth? Indicate this on the timeline.

Age in years

0 – Precambrian time begins
5 –
10 –
15 –
20 – First single-celled organism appears
25 –
30 –
35 –
40 –
45 –
50 –
55 –
60 –
65 –
70 – Paleozoic era begins
75 – Mesozoic era begins
80 – Cenozoic era begins

On this scale, Precambrian time lasts for 70 years, the Paleozoic era lasts for 5 years, the Mesozoic era lasts for 3 years, and the Cenozoic era has lasted for 1 year.

The person will be about 20 when the first single-celled organism appears.

Name ______________________ Date ____________ Class ____________

CHAPTER 9 REINFORCEMENT WORKSHEET

Condensed History

Complete this worksheet after you finish reading Chapter 9, Section 2.
Many important events that have occurred since the Earth was formed are listed below. Fill in the diagram below, listing the events in chronological order.

Prokaryotes form.

Cells with nuclei form.

Began 65 million years ago

First birds appear.

Large mammals appear.

The ozone layer develops.

Dinosaurs dominate the Earth.

Plants become established on land.

Humans appear.

Crawling insects appear on land.

Many reptile species evolve.

Organisms suffer largest mass extinction known.

Small mammals survive mass extinction.

Began 540 million years ago

Cyanobacteria begin photosynthesis and produce oxygen.

Began 4.6 billion years ago

Winged insects appear.

Began 248 million years ago

Precambrian Time
Began 4.6 billion years ago
Prokaryotes form.
Cyanobacteria begin photosynthesis and produce oxygen.
The ozone layer develops.
Cells with nuclei form.

Paleozoic Era
Began 540 million years ago
Plants become established on land.
Crawling insects appear on land.
Winged insects appear.
Organisms suffer largest mass extinction known.

Mesozoic Era
Began 248 million years ago
Many reptile species evolve.
Dinosaurs dominate the Earth.
First birds appear.
Small mammals survive mass extinction.

Cenozoic Era
Began 65 million years ago
Large mammals appear.
Humans appear.

Name ______________________ Date __________ Class __________

CHAPTER 9 **VOCABULARY REVIEW WORKSHEET**

Mary Leakey's Search

Try this puzzle after you finish Chapter 9.
Solve each of the clues below, and write your answer in the spaces provided. Then complete the quotation by Mary Leakey on the next page by writing the letter that corresponds to each number in the empty boxes.

1. large mammals evolved during this era.
   C E N[5] O Z O[6] I C
2. scientist who uses fossils to reconstruct what happened in Earth's history
   P A L E O[8] N T O[10] L O G[33] I[31] S T
3. measuring the ratio of unstable to stable atoms in a rock sample to estimate the age of the fossil it contains
   A[24] B[52] S O[28] L U[23] T E D[17] A T[48] I N G
4. the first true cells
   P R O K[4] A R Y[1] O[35] T E[53] S
5. cells that contain a nucleus
   E U[9] K[30] A R Y[42] O[56] T E S
6. scientist who discovered fossilized footprints in Tanzania
   M A R Y[13] L[41] E A K[54] E Y[7]
7. hominid that lived in Germany 230,000 years ago
   N[16] E A N D E R[37] T H[51] A L
8. an imprint of a living thing preserved in rock
   F[14] O S S I L[12]
9. Lucy is the most complete example of a(n) ________ ever found.
   A U[3] S T R[36] A L O P I T H[18] E C I N[32] E
10. When a species dies out completely, it becomes ________.
   E[38] X T I[15] N C T[20]
11. the theory that explains how the continents move
   P L[27] A T[50] E T E[47] C T O N[11] I C S

Name ______________________ Date __________ Class __________

Mary Leakey's Search, continued

12. a group of mammals with binocular vision and opposable thumbs
   P R[49] I M A T[45] E S
13. Humans and their human-like ancestors are called ________.
   H[46] O M I N[55] I D S
14. organisms that don't need oxygen to survive
   A N A[39] E R[25] O B I C
15. a gas that absorbs ultraviolet radiation
   O[2] Z O N[57] E
16. the single landmass that existed about 245 million years ago
   P A[19] N G A E[26] A
17. The first birds appeared during this era.
   M E S O[29] Z O I[43] C
18. During this era, the first land-dwelling organisms appeared.
   P A L[40] E O[22] Z O I C
19. the process by which one type of rock changes into another type of rock
   R O C K C Y[21] C L E
20. the time it takes for half of the unstable atoms in a sample to decay
   H A L F[34] - L I F[44] E

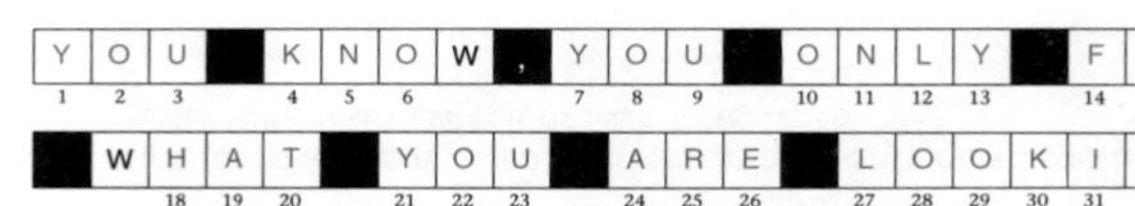

— Mary Leakey, 1994

Name ______________________ Date ____________ Class ____________

Keys to the Kingdom, continued

Animalia	Plantae
Most possess a nervous system *Felis domesticus* All have cells that lack cell walls	Usually green Use the sun's energy to make sugar Ferns

Protista	Fungi
Most are single-celled organisms All eukaryotes that are not plants, animals, or fungi Algae Evolved from bacteria about 2 billion years ago	Break down material outside their bodies and then absorb the nutrients Molds Mushrooms

Eubacteria	Archaebacteria
Escherichia coli Prokaryotes that may be found in the human body All are single-celled organisms Do not have nuclei	Have existed for at least 3 billion years Form yellow rings around hot springs where the temperature is 90°C All are single-celled organisms Do not have nuclei

Name ______________________ Date ____________ Class ____________

CHAPTER 10 VOCABULARY REVIEW WORKSHEET

Classification Clues

Complete this puzzle after you have finished Chapter 10.

Solve the clues to see what words are hidden in the puzzle. Words in the puzzle are hidden vertically, horizontally, and diagonally.

1. List the seven levels used by scientists to classify organisms in order from most general to least general.

a. kingdom

b. phylum

c. class

d. order

e. family

f. genus

g. species

2. For each of the following descriptions, write the kingdom of the organisms being described in the space provided.

a. Eubacteria — Single-celled organisms without nuclei, such as *Escherichia coli,* which live in the human body

b. Plantae — Multicellular eukaryotic organisms that are usually green and make sugar through photosynthesis

c. Archaebacteria — Unicellular prokaryotes that have been on Earth for at least 3 billion years

d. Animalia — Multicellular organisms whose cells have nuclei but do not have cell walls

e. Fungi — Multicellular organisms that have cells containing nuclei and that absorb nutrients from their surroundings after breaking them down with digestive juices

f. Protista — Single-celled or multicellular eukaryotic organisms that are not plants, animals, or fungi

3. Linnaeus founded taxonomy, the science of identifying, naming, and classifying living things.

4. A dichotomous key is a special guide used to identify unknown organisms.

Name ________________ Date ________ Class ________

Classification Clues, continued

A	O	D	R	P	H	Y	L	U	M	X	O	B	K
M	R	I	O	K	N	A	R	I	P	P	H	Y	Y
O	E	C	M	R	E	H	O	C	M	L	Y	M	T
D	R	H	H	O	D	F	N	S	I	A	O	D	C
G	A	O	I	A	G	E	S	C	A	N	M	S	L
N	L	T	K	B	E	U	R	T	O	T	S	P	E
I	Q	O	I	U	N	B	E	X	S	A	U	E	U
K	H	M	Y	L	U	T	A	D	L	E	E	C	G
P	R	O	T	I	S	T	A	C	P	S	A	I	S
A	Y	U	T	I	E	B	D	R	T	E	R	E	F
I	L	S	G	U	V	O	G	U	C	E	H	S	O
Z	U	N	A	E	U	B	A	C	T	E	R	I	A
M	U	G	T	F	N	W	P	L	R	B	S	I	Y
F	A	M	I	L	Y	A	N	I	M	A	L	I	A

Name ________________ Date ________ Class ________

CHAPTER 11 REINFORCEMENT WORKSHEET

Classifying Plants

Complete this worksheet after you finish reading Chapter 11, Section 3.

Each of the boxes below represents one of the main groups of living plants. Write the descriptions given at the bottom of the page in the appropriate box. Some descriptions may be used more than once.

Nonvascular plants	Vascular plants without seeds
mosses and liverworts must obtain water by osmosis have rhizoids instead of roots usually the first plants to inhabit a new, bare environment	ferns, horsetails, and club mosses ancestors grew very large formed fossil fuels contain xylem and phloem to transport water and food
Vascular plants with seeds but without flowers	**Vascular plants with seeds and flowers**
gymnosperms conifers are an example seeds develop in a cone or on fleshy structures attached to branches include the oldest living trees on Earth contain xylem and phloem to transport water and food	angiosperms seeds are surrounded by a fruit are the most successful group of plants today provide land animals with almost all of the food they need to survive contain xylem and phloem to transport water and food

Notes

- ancestors grew very large
- conifers are an example
- provide land animals with almost all of the food they need to survive
- include the oldest living trees on Earth
- have rhizoids instead of roots
- angiosperms
- seeds are surrounded by a fruit
- are the most successful group of plants today
- mosses and liverworts
- usually the first plants to inhabit a new, bare environment
- formed fossil fuels
- ferns, horsetails, and club mosses
- gymnosperms
- must obtain water by osmosis
- contain xylem and phloem to transport water and food
- seeds develop in a cone or on fleshy structures attached to branches

Name ______________ Date ________ Class ________

CHAPTER 11 REINFORCEMENT WORKSHEET

Drawing Dicots

Complete this worksheet after you finish reading Chapter 11, Section 3.

There are two classes of angiosperms—monocots and dicots. The main difference between the two classes is that monocots have one seed leaf and dicots have two seed leaves. However, there are other differences between them.

Below are illustrations of some of the features that distinguish monocots from dicots. Use the description of how a dicot differs from a monocot to draw the same features for a dicot.

Monocot	How is a dicot different from a monocot?	Dicot
Arrangement of vascular tissue	A monocot has bundles of vascular tissue scattered throughout the stem, while a dicot has bundles of vascular tissue arranged in a ring.	Arrangement of vascular tissue
Flower	A monocot has a flower with parts in threes, while a dicot has a flower with parts in fours or fives.	Flower
Pattern of leaf vein	A monocot has leaves with parallel veins, while a dicot has leaves with branching veins.	Pattern of leaf vein

Name ______________ Date ________ Class ________

CHAPTER 11 VOCABULARY REVIEW WORKSHEET

Those Puzzling Plants

After finishing Chapter 11, give this puzzle a try!

Solve each of the clues below, and write your answer in the spaces provided.

1. spore-producing stage of a plant
   S P O R O P H Y T E (24)
2. plants with specialized tissue to move materials from one part of the plant to another
   V A S C U L A R (3)
3. male reproductive structure in a flower
   S T A M E N (12)
4. dustlike particles produced in the anthers of flowers
   P O L L E N (19)
5. small, hairlike threads of cells that keep mosses grounded
   R H I Z O I D S (14)
6. openings in the epidermis of a leaf that let CO_2 into the leaves
   S T O M A T A (20)
7. plant "pipes" that transport sugar molecules
   P H L O E M (2)
8. waxy layer that coats the surface of stems and leaves
   C U T I C L E (18)
9. structures that cover immature flowers
   S E P A L S (5, 26)
10. usually obtains water close to the soil surface
    F I B R O U S R O O T (25, 9)
11. nonflowering, seed-producing plants
    G Y M N O S P E R M S (8)
12. part of a flower that contains the ovules
    O V A R Y (1)

Name ______________________ Date ____________ Class ____________

Those Puzzling Plants, continued

13. seed leaf inside a seed
C O T Y L E D(11) O N(13)

14. attract pollinators to the flower
P E T A(22) L S

15. outermost layer of cells that covers roots, stems, leaves, and flower parts
E P I D E R(7) M I S

16. plants that have no "pipes" to transport materials from one part of the plant to another
N O N V(15) A S C U(27) L A R

17. seed-producing plants with flowers
A N G I O S P E R(23) M S

18. plant "pipes" that transport water and minerals
X Y L E(10) M

19. can obtain water that is deep underground
T A P R O(17) O T

20. plant stage that produces sex cells
G A(6) M E(28) T O P H Y T E

21. tip of the pistil; collects pollen
S(21) T I G M A

22. underground stem of a fern
R H I Z O M E(4)

23. female reproductive structure in a flower
P I S T I(16) L

Write the letter that corresponds to each number in the empty boxes to form the beginning of a well-known poem.

R	O	S	E	S	■	A	R	E	■	R	E	D	■	A	N	D
1	2	3	4	5		6	7	8		9	10	11		12	13	14

V	I	O	L	E	T	S	■	A	R	E	■	B	L	U	E
15	16	17	18	19	20	21		22	23	24		25	26	27	28

Name ______________________ Date ____________ Class ____________

CHAPTER 12 **REINFORCEMENT WORKSHEET**

Fertilizing Flowers

Complete this worksheet after you finish reading Chapter 12, Section 1.

Flowers are adaptations that plants use for sexual reproduction.

1. Below is a cross section of a flower. Label the parts of the flower by writing each of the terms in the appropriate space.

TERMS
- sepal
- anther
- ovary
- pollen
- stigma
- style
- petal

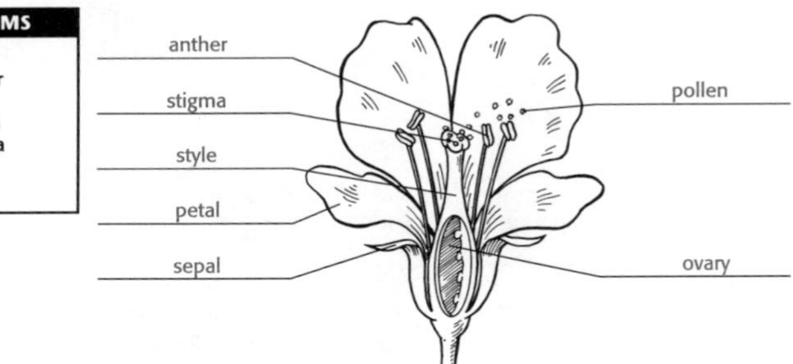

2. For fertilization to occur, a sperm has to reach the egg. Use the terms in the box below to label the following illustration, which shows how a sperm cell fuses with an egg in a flower.

TERMS
- egg within an ovule
- sperm cell
- pollen tube
- ovary

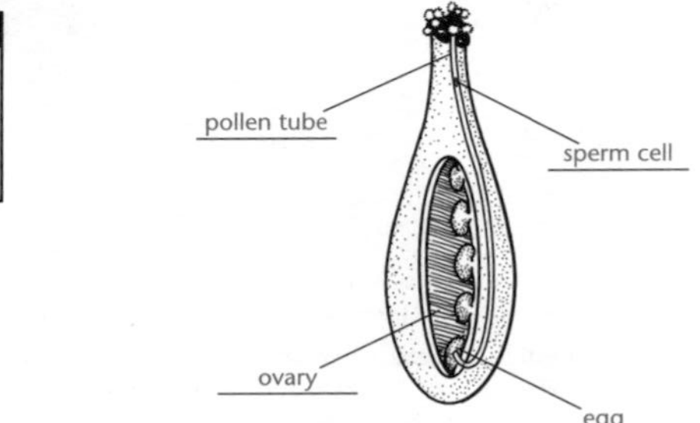

3. In the illustration above, which structure turns into the fruit after fertilization?

The ovary turns into the fruit after fertilization.

Name ______________________ Date ____________ Class ____________

CHAPTER 12 REINFORCEMENT WORKSHEET

A Leaf's Work Is Never Done

Complete this worksheet after you finish reading Chapter 12, Section 2.

A plant makes food in its leaves. Complete the outline below by filling in the blanks in the diagram with the words at the bottom of the page.

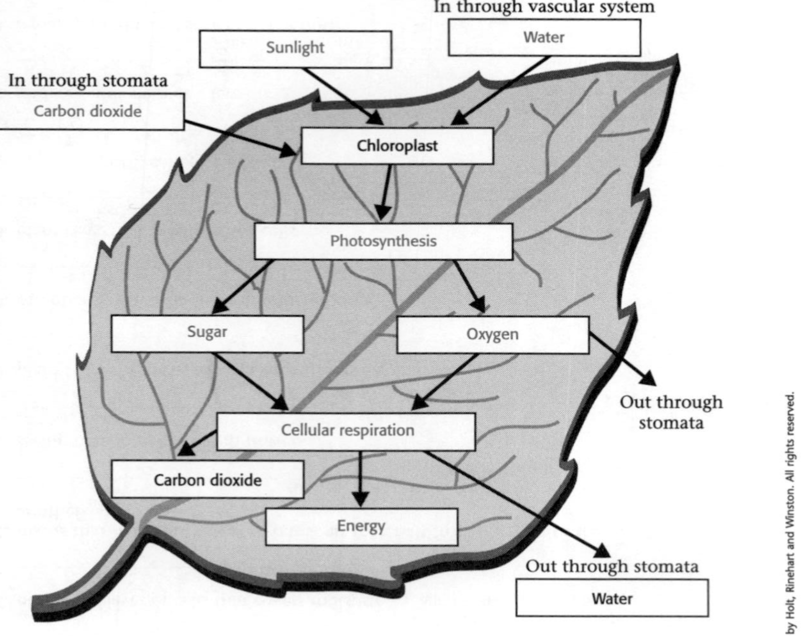

Words

- photosynthesis
- cellular respiration
- sugar
- carbon dioxide
- water
- oxygen
- sunlight
- energy

Name ______________________ Date ____________ Class ____________

CHAPTER 12 REINFORCEMENT WORKSHEET

How Plants Respond to Change

Complete this worksheet after you finish reading Chapter 12, Section 3.

Although plants don't walk and talk, they do respond to stimuli in their environment. Plants respond to stimuli by growing in a particular direction. Plant growth away from a stimulus is a negative tropism. Plant growth toward a stimulus is a positive tropism.

1. The plant shown below has just been moved next to a window from a room with no direct light. Sketch what the plant will look like in a few days.

In a few days

2. Phototropism is a change in the growth of a plant in response to light. Is phototropism positive or negative?

Phototropism is positive.

3. The plant shown below has just been tipped over on its side. Sketch what the plant will look like in a few days. (Hint: The plant will respond to gravity.)

In a few days

4. Gravitropism is a change in the direction of the growth of a plant in response to gravity. Is gravitropism of most shoot tips positive or negative?

Gravitropism of most shoot tips is negative.

Name ______________ Date ________ Class ________

CHAPTER 12 VOCABULARY REVIEW WORKSHEET

Scrambled Plants

After you finish Chapter 12, try this puzzle!

Use the clues to unscramble each of the words below, and write the word in the space provided.

	Scrambled	Clue	Answer
1.	IOSDDUUEC	a tree that loses all of its leaves at the same time each year	D E (C) I D U O U S
2.	TAOTSMA	the openings in a leaf's epidermis that allow carbon dioxide in and oxygen and water out	S T O M (A) T A
3.	OISRMTP	a change in a plant's growth in response to a stimulus	T R O P I (S) M
4.	NEREGEVER	a tree that keeps its leaves year-round	E V E (R) G R E E N
5.	OORMHNE	a chemical messenger that carries information from one part of an organism to another	(H) O R M O N E
6.	VAPMTGROSIIR	a change in the direction a plant grows in response to gravity	G R A V I T R O (P) I S M
7.	MOPTOPSIRHOT	a change in the way a plant grows in response to light	P H O T (O) T R O P I S M
8.	EUALCRLL EAPRRIINOST (two words)	the process that converts the energy stored in food into a form cells can use	C E (L) L U (L) A R / R E S P I R A T I O N
9.	AAIINNTTRRSPO	the loss of water from leaves	T R A N S P I R A (T) I O N
10.	TRODNAM	inactive state of a seed	D (O) R M A N T

Now unscramble the circled letters to find the organelle that contains the photosynthetic pigment in plants.

C H L O R O P L A S T

Name ______________ Date ________ Class ________

CHAPTER 13 REINFORCEMENT WORKSHEET

What Makes an Animal an Animal?

Complete this worksheet after reading Chapter 13, Section 1.

Whales, armadillos, hummingbirds, spiders… animals come in all shapes and sizes. Not all animals have backbones, and not all animals have hair. So what makes an animal an animal?

Complete the chart below by using the words and phrases at the bottom of the page.

Animal Characteristics

Animal Characteristics
- move
- are consumers
- have specialized parts
  - tissues
    - organs
- reproduce
  - sexually
    - fertilized egg cell
      - develop from embryos
  - asexually
    - budding
    - division
- multicellular
  - cells are eukaryotic
  - cells have no cell walls

Words and Phrases

- move
- budding
- develop from embryos
- have specialized parts
- sexually
- asexually
- multicellular
- cells have no cell walls
- division
- are consumers

Name ____________ Date ________ Class ________

CHAPTER 13 **REINFORCEMENT WORKSHEET**

Animal Interviews

Complete this worksheet after reading Chapter 13, Section 2.

Imagine that you work with Dr. Phishtof Finz, a researcher who can really talk to the animals. Below are some sections of his taped animal interviews. Your job is to decide what animal behavior or characteristic is being described and to write it in the space provided. Possible answers are *warning coloration, migration, hibernation, estivation,* and *camouflage.*

Interviewed animal		Behavior or characteristic
Canada goose:	During the summer, we stay up in Canada. It's really a nice place in summer, with lots of food and lots of sun. But before the snow starts to fly, we high-tail it south!	migration
Arctic ground squirrel:	What's the winter like in Alaska? Strange, I really don't know. I spend all summer eating and getting my nest ready, but then during the fall I get so sleepy! I go to bed and—*poof!*—when I wake up it's spring!	hibernation
Desert mouse:	Oh, living in the desert is wonderful! I love sunshine. During the really hot part of the summer, of course, I stay inside my nest, and I nap a lot. It's so much cooler inside.	estivation
Ladybug:	Thank you! I am a lovely shade of red, aren't I? But just between you and me, did you know that this beautiful color tells birds that I am, well, rather nasty tasting?	warning coloration
Chameleon:	Yoo-hoo! I'm over here! See? In the potted plant. Well, yes, I am rather proud of being able to turn that particular shade of green. Not all animals can do that, you know.	camouflage

Name ____________ Date ________ Class ________

Puzzling Animal Behavior, continued

Across: 3 NAVIGATE; 4 CONSUMER; 6 LEARNED; 7 EMBRYO; 8 MIGRATE; 10 BIOLOGICAL CLOCK; 16 TERRITORY; 18 SOCIAL; 19 PREDATOR; 20 MULTICELLULAR; 21 HIBERNATION

Down: 1 PHEROMONES; 2 INVERTEBRATE; 5 CAMOUFLAGE; 7 ESTIVATION; 9 TISSUE; 11 ORGAN; 12 COMMUNICATION; 13 LANDMARK; 14 CIRCADIAN; 15 VERTEBRATE; 17 INNATE; 22 PREY

Name ____________ Date ________ Class ________

CHAPTER 14 REINFORCEMENT WORKSHEET

Life Without a Backbone

Complete this worksheet after you finish reading Chapter 14, Section 1.

What do a butterfly, a spider, a jellyfish, a worm, a snail, an octopus, and a lobster have in common? All of these animals are invertebrates. Clearly, there are many differences between these animals. Yet the most important characteristic these animals share is something none of them have—a backbone!

Despite their obvious differences, all invertebrates share some basic characteristics. Using the list of words provided, fill in the boxes with the correct answers. There will be some words that you will not use at all.

Characteristics

spicules
asymmetry
ganglia
gut
nerve cord
bilateral symmetry
collar cells
neutron
uniform
nerve networks
radial symmetry

All About Invertebrates

An invertebrate has a body plan that can have

asymmetry

bilateral symmetry

radial symmetry

An invertebrate might use these structures to digest its food.

gut

collar cells

An invertebrate might use one or more of the following structures to control its body movement.

nerve networks

ganglia

nerve cord

Name ____________ Date ________ Class ________

CHAPTER 14 REINFORCEMENT WORKSHEET

Spineless Variety

Complete this worksheet after you finish reading Chapter 14, Section 4.

In each of the four completed lists, seven phrases were accidentally placed in the wrong list. Those seven phrases describe Annelid Worms. Circle the phrases that were placed incorrectly in the complete lists, and use those phrases to complete the list for Annelid Worms.

Echinoderms

live only in the ocean
(have a brain)
have an endoskeleton
have a nerve ring
are covered with spines or bumps
some have a radial nerve
have a water vascular system
sand dollar
sea urchin
(a bristle worm)

Annelid Worms

have a closed circulatory system
have a brain
have a nerve cord
have segments
a leech
an earthworm
a bristle worm

Arthropods

have a well-developed brain
have jointed limbs
have a head
have an exoskeleton
have a well-developed nervous system
a tick
(an earthworm)
a dragonfly

Mollusks

live in the ocean, fresh water, or land
have open or closed circulatory system
have a foot and a mantle
usually have a shell
have a visceral mass
have complex ganglia
(a leech)
a clam
a snail
(have segments)

Cnidarians

live in the ocean or fresh water
(have a nerve cord)
have a gut
have a nerve net
are in polyp or medusa form
have stinging cells
a jellyfish
a sea anemone
coral
(have a closed circulatory system)

Name ____________________ Date __________ Class __________

CHAPTER 14 VOCABULARY REVIEW WORKSHEET

Searching for a Backbone

After you finish Chapter 14, give this puzzle a try!
Identify the word described by each clue, and write the word in the space provided. Then circle the word in the puzzle on the next page.

1. external body-support structure made of protein and chitin — exoskeleton
2. combination of head and thorax — cephalothorax
3. type of circulatory system in which blood is pumped through a network of vessels that form a closed loop — closed
4. symmetry in which an organism's body has two halves that are mirror images of each other — bilateral
5. groups of nerve cells — ganglia
6. identical or almost identical repeating body parts — segments
7. form of cnidarian that looks like a mushroom with tentacles — medusa
8. an animal without a backbone — invertebrate
9. vase-shaped form of cnidarian — polyp
10. type of circulatory system in which blood is pumped through spaces called sinuses — open
11. the process through which an insect develops from an egg to an adult while changing form — metamorphosis
12. without symmetry — asymmetrical
13. three specialized parts of arthropods formed when two or three segments grow together
    a. head
    b. thorax
    c. abdomen
14. symmetry in which an organism's body parts are arranged in a circle around a central point — radial
15. eye made of many identical light-sensitive cells — compound
16. pouch where almost all animals digest food — gut
17. jaws found on some arthropods — mandibles

Name ____________________ Date __________ Class __________

18. the space in the body where the gut is located — coelom
19. an organism that feeds on another organism, usually without killing it — parasite
20. feelers that respond to touch or taste — antennae
21. internal body-support structure — endoskeleton
22. organism on which the organism in item 19 lives — host
23. system that allows echinoderms to move, eat, and breathe — water vascular

M	K	D	J	P	F	B	I	L	A	T	E	R	A	L	T	A
X	E	N	D	O	S	K	E	L	E	T	O	N	P	S	K	N
F	B	T	C	O	E	L	O	M	Y	E	P	V	O	E	X	T
P	A	G	A	A	S	U	D	E	M	L	E	H	F	T	M	E
I	Q	S	H	M	Z	O	W	A	Q	V	N	X	E	I	R	N
N	V	E	Y	K	O	D	A	N	I	P	A	X	J	S	A	N
V	G	L	L	M	P	R	E	A	G	R	O	N	S	A	L	A
E	X	B	N	X	M	M	P	M	O	S	Q	L	O	R	U	E
R	D	I	A	V	O	E	D	H	K	A	W	R	Y	A	C	F
T	L	D	W	D	B	N	T	E	O	B	P	X	G	P	S	S
E	A	N	B	A	P	O	L	R	D	S	A	R	A	M	A	E
B	S	A	O	C	L	E	J	E	I	R	I	W	N	S	V	G
R	E	M	P	A	T	G	S	G	O	C	P	S	G	U	R	M
A	D	E	H	O	B	O	X	H	U	K	A	X	L	N	E	E
T	A	P	N	X	L	Q	T	N	Z	T	S	L	I	V	T	N
E	E	J	P	C	O	M	P	O	U	N	D	O	A	Z	A	T
C	H	Z	G	F	R	I	L	A	I	D	A	R	T	U	W	S

Name ______________________ Date __________ Class __________

Coldblooded Critters, continued

Coldblooded Critter Chart

Amphibians	metamorphosis eggs laid in water no scales vertebrates consumers thin, moist skin ectotherms "double life" breathe through skin and lungs external or internal fertilization almost all adults have lungs many have bright colors to scare predators
Reptiles	ectotherms consumers only internal fertilization amniotic egg most lay eggs on land thick, dry skin vertebrates breathe through lungs some have young born live many have scales
Fishes	vertebrates mostly external fertilization gills fins many have scales many have swim bladders ectotherms consumers lateral line system some have skeletons of cartilage some have young born live eggs laid in water

Name ______________________ Date __________ Class __________

Fishin' for Vertebrates, continued

1 REPTILES
6 LATERAL LINE
8 LIVER
9 BONY
10 TADPOLE
11 SWIM BLADDER
14 ENDOTHERM
16 SCALES
21 GILLS
22 THERAPSID
23 SING
24 RAYS
25 TORTOISES

2 INTERNAL
3 EXTERNAL
4 JAWLESS
5 ECTOTHERM
7 AMNIOTIC
12 DENTICLES
13 METAMORPHOSIS
15 CARTILAGINOUS
17 LUNGS
18 VERTEBRATE
19 LUNGFISHES
20 FIN

Name ______________ Date ______________ Class ______________

CHAPTER 16 REINFORCEMENT WORKSHEET

Mammals Are Us

Complete this worksheet after you finish reading Chapter 16, Section 2.
Each of the following terms is either an order of animals or an example of a particular order. Use the characteristics and facts in the table below to identify the order and one example of each group of animals, and record the corresponding terms in the spaces provided.

dolphin	cetaceans	hoofed mammals	sirenia
rabbit	human	carnivores	rodents
porcupine	aardvark	cow	toothless mammals
primates	manatee	Siberian tiger	
insectivores	lagomorphs	hedgehog	

Order	Characteristic	Example	An interesting fact
toothless mammals	generally eat insects and have long, sticky tongues	aardvark	only one is truly "toothless"
insectivores	tend to have pointed noses for digging	hedgehog	live on all continents but Australia
rodents	small animals that have sharp front teeth for gnawing	porcupine	front teeth never stop growing
lagomorphs	have strong legs for jumping, sensitive noses, and big ears	rabbit	some gather plants and shape them in "haystacks" to dry
primates	have eyes that face forward and oppos-able thumbs	human	considered the most intelligent mammals
carnivores	eat mostly meat	Siberian tiger	some handle food like monkeys do
hoofed mammals	generally fast runners; they have flat teeth for chewing plants	cow	divided into groups according to the number of toes
cetaceans	water-dwelling mammals that resemble fish	dolphin	use echolocation like bats do
sirenia	eat seaweed and water plants	manatee	only four species in this order

Name ______________ Date ______________ Class ______________

CHAPTER 16 VOCABULARY REVIEW WORKSHEET

Is It a Bird or a Mammal?

Complete this worksheet after you finish reading Chapter 16.
Match each description in the second column with the correct term in the first column, and write the corresponding letter in the space provided.

d 1. primates
j 2. contour feathers
i 3. carnivores
k 4. down feathers
c 5. gestation period
n 6. preening
f 7. placenta
m 8. lift
b 9. placental mammals
p 10. brooding
q 11. marsupials
o 12. precocial chicks
g 13. monotremes
e 14. altricial chicks
h 15. therapsids
l 16. mammary glands
a 17. diaphragm

a. a large muscle at the bottom of the rib cage that helps bring air into the lungs
b. a mammal that nourishes its unborn offspring with a special organ inside the uterus
c. the time during which an embryo develops within the mother
d. a group of mammals that have opposable thumbs and binocular vision; includes humans, apes, and monkeys
e. chicks that hatch weak, naked, and helpless
f. a special organ of exchange that provides a developing fetus with nutrients and oxygen
g. mammals that lay eggs
h. prehistoric reptile ancestors of mammals
i. consumers that eat animals
j. feathers made of a stiff central shaft with many side branches called barbs
k. fluffy, insulating feathers that lie next to a bird's body
l. glands that secrete a nutritious fluid called milk
m. the upward pressure on the wing of a bird that keeps a bird in the air
n. when a bird uses its beak to spread oil on its feathers
o. chicks that hatch fully active
p. when a bird sits on its eggs until they hatch
q. a mammal that gives birth to partially developed, live young that develop inside the mother's pouch or skin fold

Name ______________ Date ________ Class ________

CHAPTER 17 **REINFORCEMENT WORKSHEET**

Know Your Biomes

Complete this worksheet after you have finished reading Chapter 17, Section 1.

1. Using the Temperature & rainfall column as a guide, label the biomes using the following terms: *desert, tropical rain forest, arctic tundra, coniferous forest, temperate grassland, savanna,* and *temperate deciduous forest.*
2. Use the examples and characteristics given in the box on the next page to fill in the appropriate blanks.

Type of biome	Temperature & rainfall	Examples & characteristics
desert	summer: 38°C winter: 7°C rain: less than 25 cm per year	jack rabbit most animals are active at night plants spaced far apart
savanna	dry season: 34°C wet season: 16°C rain: 150 cm per year	has scattered clumps of trees diverse groups of herbivores live here giraffe
tropical rain forest	daytime: 34°C nighttime: 20°C rain: up to 400 cm per year	the most biologically diverse biome animals prefer life in the treetops most nutrients in the vegetation
temperate deciduous forest	summer: 28°C winter: 6°C rain: 75–125 cm per year	woody shrubs beneath tree layer woodpecker trees lose leaves in fall

Name ______________ Date ________ Class ________

Type of biome	Temperature & rainfall	Examples & characteristics
arctic tundra	summer: 12°C winter: −26°C rain: 30–50 cm per year	has no trees permafrost musk ox
coniferous forest	summer: 14°C winter: −10°C rain: 35–75 cm per year	waxy coating on needles trees produce seed in cones porcupine
temperate grassland	summer: 30°C winter: 0°C rain: 25–75 cm per year	has few slow-growing plants very few trees bison

EXAMPLES AND CHARACTERISTICS

musk ox
bison
giraffe
woodpecker
porcupine
animals prefer life in the treetops
most animals are active at night
trees produce seeds in cones
very few trees
plants spaced far apart
permafrost
trees lose leaves in fall
diverse groups of herbivores live here
most nutrients in the vegetation

Name ______________ Date ______ Class ______

CHAPTER 17 **VOCABULARY REVIEW WORKSHEET**

Eco-Puzzle

After you finish Chapter 17, give this puzzle a try!
In the space provided, write the term described by the clue. Then find those words in the puzzle. Terms can be hidden in the puzzle vertically, horizontally, or diagonally.

1. a biome in the far north where no trees can grow
tundra
2. a tree that produces seeds in a cone conifer
3. soil that is always frozen permafrost
4. a hot, dry biome that receives less than 25 cm of rain a year
desert
5. the zone of a lake or pond closest to the edge of the land
littoral
6. a treeless wetland ecosystem marsh
7. microscopic photosynthetic organisms in the ocean
phytoplankton
8. geographic area characterized by certain types of plants and animals biome
9. trees that lose their leaves in the fall
deciduous
10. a wetland ecosystem with trees swamp
11. an algae that forms rafts in the Sargasso Sea
Sargassum
12. an area where fresh and salty waters constantly mix
estuary
13. land where the water level is near or above the surface of the ground for most of the year wetland
14. very small consumers in the ocean zooplankton
15. a tropical grassland with scattered clumps of trees
savanna
16. a small stream or river that flows into a larger one
tributary
17. nonliving factors in the environment
abiotic

Name ______________ Date ______ Class ______

Eco-Puzzle, continued

18. a measure of the number of species an area contains
diversity

T	S	O	N	O	D	E	S	E	R	T	A	R	I	N	Z	X
U	V	C	W	T	R	I	B	U	E	Z	P	C	H	O	V	G
N	B	Q	E	F	E	G	C	L	L	I	T	T	O	R	A	L
D	L	S	T	S	O	R	F	A	M	R	E	P	Q	U	L	B
R	H	A	L	P	E	M	A	F	P	O	L	N	B	K	S	C
A	O	V	A	R	C	X	S	A	R	A	O	J	T	W	G	F
P	Y	D	N	D	V	F	J	C	N	T	G	O	A	Y	E	D
H	R	I	D	E	A	R	W	K	K	Y	N	M	C	M	H	S
Y	A	V	R	C	L	S	T	N	B	L	P	Z	O	X	L	A
T	U	E	M	I	Q	O	A	G	Q	C	I	I	N	K	Z	N
O	T	R	Y	D	N	L	P	R	M	O	B	T	I	R	O	N
P	S	S	C	U	P	I	B	E	G	K	F	V	F	Q	O	A
Z	E	I	Q	O	M	W	E	T	L	A	T	B	E	J	P	V
A	G	T	T	U	N	D	L	F	D	O	S	G	R	L	L	A
I	W	Y	R	S	C	I	T	O	I	B	A	S	O	N	B	S
V	H	E	A	B	M	A	R	S	H	N	D	L	U	W	T	E
P	D	J	L	C	Y	R	A	T	U	B	I	R	T	M	N	V

Name ______________ Date ________ Class ________

CHAPTER 18 VOCABULARY REVIEW WORKSHEET

Solve the Environmental Puzzle

Give this puzzle a try after you finish Chapter 18.
Using each of the clues below, fill in the letters of the term described in the blanks provided on the next page.

1. can be broken down by the environment
2. process of transforming garbage into electricity
3. type of hazardous wastes that take hundreds or thousands of years to become harmless
4. when the number of individuals becomes so large that they can't get all the resources they need
5. the process of making new products from reprocessed used products
6. the clearing of forest lands
7. the world around us
8. an organism that makes a home for itself in a new place
9. harmful substances in the environment
10. a girl who developed a way to make paper without cutting down a tree
11. describes a natural resource that can be used and replaced over a relatively short time
12. describes a natural resource that cannot be replaced or can be replaced only after thousands or millions of years
13. substances used to kill crop-destroying insects
14. the preservation of resources
15. the number and variety of living things
16. poisonous
17. the presence of harmful substances in the environment
18. protective layer of the atmosphere destroyed by CFCs

Name ______________ Date ________ Class ________

Solve the Environmental Puzzle, continued

1. B I O D E G **R** A D A B L E
2. R E S O U R C E   R E C O V E R Y
3. R A **D** I O A C T I V E
4. O V E R P O P **U** L A T I O N
5. R E **C** Y C L I N G
6. D E F O R **E** S T A T I O N
7. E N V I **R** O N M E N T
8. A L I **E** N
9. P O L L **U** T A N T S
10. H A I F A   A L D O R A **S** I
11. R E N **E** W A B L E
12. N O N **R** E N E W A B L E
13. P **E** S T I C I D E S
14. **C** O N S E R V A T I O N
15. B I O D I V E R S I T **Y**
16. T O X I **C**
17. P O **L** L U T I O N
18. O Z O N **E**

Name ______________ Date ________ Class ________

CHAPTER 19 REINFORCEMENT WORKSHEET

The Hipbone's Connected to the . . .

Complete this worksheet after you finish reading Chapter 19, Section 2.

Your skeleton makes it possible for you to move. It provides your organs with protection, stores minerals, makes white and red blood cells, and supports your body. Look at the human skeleton below, and write the names of the major bones listed below in the spaces provided.

Bones

- humerus
- fibula
- pelvic girdle
- radius
- patella
- ulna
- ribs
- skull
- clavicle
- vertebral column
- femur
- tibia

skull
clavicle
ribs
humerus
vertebral column
pelvic girdle
radius
ulna
femur
patella
fibula
tibia

The place where two or more bones connect is called a joint. In the chapter, you looked at fixed, ball-and-socket, and hinge joints.

1. What kind of joint is the elbow?

   The elbow is a hinge joint.

2. What kind of joint allows the arm to move freely in all directions?

   A ball-and-socket joint, the shoulder, allows the arm to move freely in all directions.

Name ______________ Date ________ Class ________

CHAPTER 19 REINFORCEMENT WORKSHEET

Muscle Map

Complete this worksheet after you finish reading Chapter 19, Section 3.

Each of the boxes below represents one of the three types of muscle tissue in your body. Write the notes in the appropriate box. Some of the notes can be used more than once.

Three Types of Muscle

Skeletal	Cardiac	Smooth
moves bones involuntary voluntary often work in pairs	in the heart involuntary	in blood vessels in the digestive tract involuntary

Notes

- moves bones
- involuntary
- voluntary
- often works in pairs
- in the heart
- in blood vessels
- in the digestive tract

Look at the diagram of a human leg below. A flexor is a muscle that bends a part of your body when it contracts, and an extensor is a muscle that extends a part of your body when it contracts. Label the flexor muscle and the extensor muscle on the diagram below.

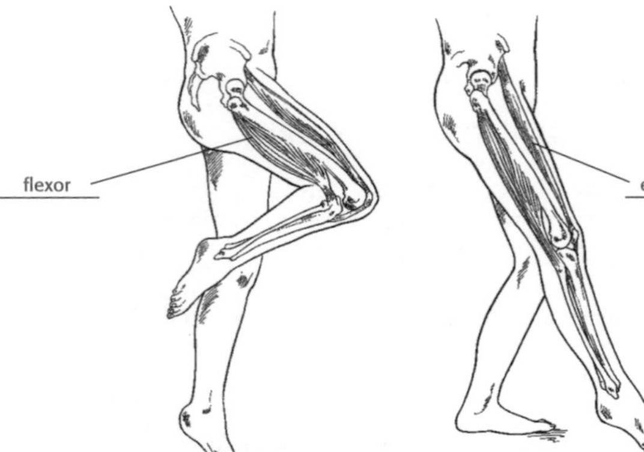

Name ______________________ Date ____________ Class ____________

A Connective Crossword, continued

Across

3. COMPACTBONE
8. JOINT
10. SWEATGLANDS
11. SPONGYBONE
17. INTEGUMENTARYSYSTEM
21. LIGAMENTS
22. HAIRFOLLICLES
23. TISSUE
24. MUSCLETISSUE
25. NERVOUS

Down

1. ORGAN
2. CARTILAGE
3. CONNECTIVETISSUE
4. EPIDERMIS
5. EXTENSOR
6. HOMEOSTASIS
7. TENDONS
9. SMOOTHMUSCLE
12. EPITHELIALTISSUE
13. FLEXOR
14. CARDIAC
15. DERMIS
16. MUSCULARSYSTEM
18. SKELETALMUSCLES
19. SKELETALSYSTEM
20. MELANIN

Name ______________________ Date ____________ Class ____________

CHAPTER 20 REINFORCEMENT WORKSHEET

Matchmaker, Matchmaker

Complete this worksheet after you finish reading Chapter 20, Section 1.

As you learned in this chapter, different blood types have different antigens and antibodies. Antigens are chemicals on the surface of red blood cells. Antibodies are chemicals in the blood's plasma. A person makes antibodies against the antigens that their red blood cells do not have. Those antibodies will attack any red blood cell that has those antigens, causing the red blood cells to clump together.

Antigens and Antibodies Present in Blood Types

Blood type	Antigens	Antibodies
O	none	A, B
A	A	B
B	B	A
AB	A, B	none

A person can receive blood from another person if the donor's blood does not contain antigens that the antibodies of the receiver's blood will attack. Complete the table below by writing *yes* or *no* in each of the blanks.

Receiver's blood type	Can receive type O?	Can receive type A?	Can receive type B?	Can receive type AB?
O	yes	no	no	no
A	yes	yes	no	no
B	yes	no	yes	no
AB	yes	yes	yes	yes

1. Which blood type do you think a hospital would find the most useful? Explain.

Sample answer: I think a hospital would find type O blood the most useful because it can be given to anyone.

Name ______________ Date ________ Class ________

CHAPTER 20 REINFORCEMENT WORKSHEET

Colors of the Heart

Complete this worksheet after you finish reading Chapter 20, Section 1.
You will need red and blue colored pencils or crayons for this worksheet.

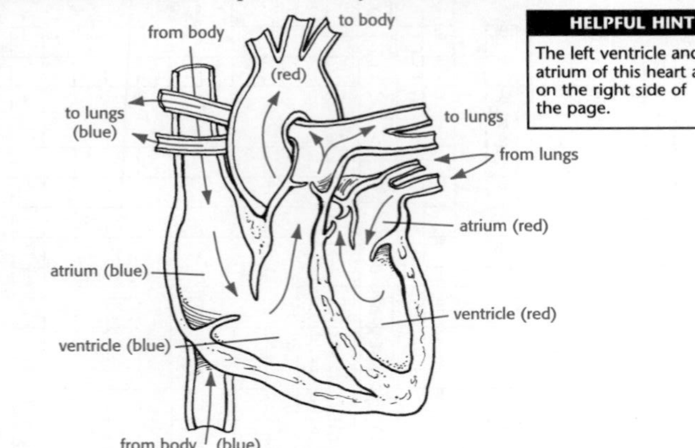

HELPFUL HINT
The left ventricle and atrium of this heart are on the right side of the page.

1. The atria are the upper chambers of the heart. The ventricles are the lower chambers of the heart. Label the atria and the ventricles on the diagram.
2. Oxygen-rich blood flows through a vein from the lungs into the left atrium. Color the left atrium and the vein that carries the blood from the lungs red.
3. Blood flows from the left atrium to the left ventricle. Color the left ventricle red.
4. Blood flows through an artery from the left ventricle to the body. The body takes up the oxygen in the blood. Color this artery red.
5. Blood flows through two large veins from the body into the right atrium. Color the right atrium and the two large veins blue.
6. Blood flows from the right atrium to the right ventricle. Color the right ventricle blue.
7. Blood flows through an artery from the right ventricle to the lungs. In the lungs, the blood picks up oxygen. Color this artery blue.
8. Add arrows to your diagram to indicate the flow of blood through the heart. Indicate whether each blood vessel is carrying blood to or from the lungs or the body.

Name ______________ Date ________ Class ________

CHAPTER 20 VOCABULARY REVIEW WORKSHEET

A Hunt with Heart

After finishing Chapter 20, give this puzzle a try!
Solve the clues below. Then use the clues to complete the puzzle on the next page.

1. cardiovascular — system that transports materials to and from the body's cells
2. blood — a connective tissue made up of cells, cell parts, and plasma
3. plasma — the fluid part of blood
4. spleen — largest lymph organ
5. pharynx — upper portion of the throat
6. lymphatic — system that collects extracellular fluid and returns it to your blood
7. thymus — lymph organ just above the heart that produces lymphocytes
8. lymph — fluid and particles absorbed into lymph capillaries
9. pulmonary — type of blood circulation between the heart and the lungs
10. capillaries — the smallest blood vessels in the body
11. larynx — your voice box
12. blood pressure — expressed in millimeters of Mercury (mm Hg)
13. platelets — cell fragments that clump together to form a plug that helps reduce blood loss
14. lymph nodes — small bean-shaped organs that remove particles from lymph
15. respiration — process that is made up of breathing and cellular respiration
16. systemic — type of blood circulation between the heart and the rest of the body
17. diaphragm — dome-shaped muscle involved in breathing
18. atria — upper heart chambers
19. arteries — blood vessels that direct blood away from the heart
20. tonsils — made up of groups of lymphatic tissue located inside your throat, at the back of your nasal cavity, and at the back of your tongue

Name ______________ Date ______ Class ______

A Hunt with Heart, continued

21. respiratory — this system consists of the lungs, the throat, and the passageways that lead to the lungs

22. ventricles — lower heart chambers

23. veins — blood vessels that direct blood toward the heart

24. alveoli — tiny sacs that form the bronchiole branches of the lungs

25. trachea — your windpipe

26. bronchi — the two tubes that connect the lungs with the trachea

How many chapter concepts can you find in the block of letters below? Use the clues to help you find them. Words may appear horizontally, vertically, diagonally, or backward.

G	L	Y	M	P	H	A	T	I	C	I	M	E	T	S	Y	S	A
T	I	A	L	V	E	O	L	I	T	O	L	N	M	O	V	L	O
O	B	S	U	R	D	S	H	U	O	C	T	E	F	O	S	Y	S
N	E	L	A	O	E	C	P	A	B	C	A	C	L	Q	Y	M	C
S	H	T	O	I	N	T	H	Y	T	A	P	L	I	M	R	P	A
I	I	L	R	O	X	Y	L	N	D	R	X	N	Y	R	A	H	P
L	B	A	R	O	D	D	T	B	I	D	I	T	R	E	N	N	I
S	Y	B	L	B	I	P	C	Y	G	I	S	A	O	S	O	O	L
E	B	M	A	R	A	L	R	S	U	O	B	O	T	P	M	D	L
L	M	L	P	R	P	A	H	E	E	V	I	X	A	I	L	E	A
C	A	H	G	H	H	T	U	I	S	A	R	L	R	R	U	S	R
I	W	R	O	R	R	E	S	R	P	S	D	T	I	A	P	U	I
R	X	N	Y	R	A	L	E	E	L	C	U	B	P	T	J	M	E
T	C	T	V	S	G	E	Y	T	E	U	P	R	S	I	E	U	S
N	C	A	N	D	M	T	K	R	E	L	I	E	E	O	S	S	R
E	P	E	P	L	A	S	M	A	N	A	Y	M	R	N	T	E	I
V	E	I	N	S	U	M	Y	H	T	R	A	C	H	E	A	Z	N

Name ______________ Date ______ Class ______

This System Is Just "Two" Nervous! continued

Left Hand: Ouch! Pain! Pain! Pain! Spinal Cord, help!

Spinal Cord: Left Hand, stop touching that hot mug!

Cerebellum: Watch out, Legs! Leg Muscles, this is the **Cerebellum**, be quick about it and step to the side, not to the back! You are about to trip over the dog!

Cerebrum: Hey, what just happened? I missed it.

Spinal Cord: Don't worry, Cerebrum, it was just another involuntary movement. The mug we grabbed was too hot to handle, so a reflex prevented the hands from getting burned. I took care of it since you are just too slow, but hey, that's my job.

Questions

1. The nervous system is made up of the ___central___ nervous system and the ___peripheral___ nervous system.
2. The central nervous system is made up of the brain and the ___spinal cord___.
3. The peripheral nervous system has many ___nerves___ throughout the body.
4. Combing your hair, getting out of bed, and getting dressed are all examples of ___voluntary movement___.
5. The process of digestion and the pumping your heart does are both examples of ___involuntary movement___.
6. The neurons in your body use ___dendrites___ and ___axons___ to transfer information.
7. The ___cerebrum___ is responsible for thinking and memory.
8. The ___medulla___ controls your heart rate, blood pressure, and involuntary breathing.
9. The ___cerebellum___ keeps track of the body's position.
10. ___Motor neurons___ tell your muscles to move.
11. Sensory neurons use ___receptors___ to tell you when you are hungry and cold.

Name ______________ Date ______ Class ______

CHAPTER 21 REINFORCEMENT WORKSHEET

The Eyes Have It

Complete this worksheet after you finish reading Chapter 21, Section 2.

Match the descriptions in Column B with the correct structure in Column A, and write the corresponding letter in the appropriate space. When you have finished, use the words in Column A to label the diagram.

Column A		Column B
b	**1.** rods	**a.** holds the photoreceptors
d	**2.** lens	**b.** give a view of the world in grays
g	**3.** optic nerve	**c.** changes pupil size to control the amount of light entering
f	**4.** cones	**d.** focuses light onto the retina
c	**5.** iris	**e.** allows light into the eye
e	**6.** pupil	**f.** interpret bright light; give a colorful view of the world
a	**7.** retina	**g.** takes impulses from the retina to the brain

Name ______________ Date ______ Class ______

CHAPTER 21 REINFORCEMENT WORKSHEET

Every Gland Lends a Hand

Complete this worksheet after you finish reading Chapter 21, Section 3.

1. How many endocrine glands are discussed in this chapter?
8

2. The parathyroid glands regulate the level of calcium in your blood.

3. Which gland controls blood-sugar levels?
pancreas

4. When your body responds to stress or danger, it uses the adrenal glands.

5. Which one of the glands helps your body fight disease?
thymus

6. Your body uses chemical messengers released into the blood, called hormones, to control body functions.

7. The thyroid gland increases the rate at which you use energy.

8. Which glands are involved in reproduction?
testes or ovaries

9. This gland has many functions, one of which is to help the thyroid function properly. Which gland is this?
pituitary

10. All these glands are part of the endocrine system.

11. What are the functions of the endocrine system?
It is involved in the control of slower, more long term processes such as fluid balance, growth, and sexual development.

Name ______________ Date ________ Class ________

CHAPTER 21 VOCABULARY REVIEW WORKSHEET

Your Body's Own Language

Give this anagram a try after you finish reading Chapter 21!

1. system in your body responsible for gathering and interpreting information about the body's internal and external environment: URSVNEO
   N E R V O U S
2. small snail-shaped organ of the inner ear: CHACOLE
   C O C H L E A
3. subdivision of question 1; includes your brain and spinal cord: ANRCELT
   C E N T R A L
4. subdivision of your nervous system; collection of nerves: LIPPERHARE
   P E R I P H E R A L
5. piece of curved material in the eye that focuses light on the retina: SLEN
   L E N S
6. specialized cells that transfer messages as electrical energy: NENORUS
   N E U R O N S
7. special neurons in your eye that help you see color: SNOCE
   C O N E S
8. short branched extensions through which question 6 receives signals: SERENDDIT
   D E N D R I T E S
9. long cell fiber that transmits information to other cells: NOXA
   A X O N
10. type of neuron that gathers information about what is happening in and around your body: NYSSREO
    S E N S O R Y
11. group of cells that makes special chemicals for your body: GNALD
    G L A N D
12. colored part of the eye: ISRI
    I R I S
13. specialized dendrites that detect changes inside or outside the body: OPETCRSER
    R E C E P T O R S

Name ______________ Date ________ Class ________

14. send messages from the brain and spinal cord to other systems: OMOTR EOSURNN
    M O T O R   N E U R O N S
15. axons that are bundled together with blood vessels and connective tissue: NSREVE
    N E R V E S
16. the largest organ of the central nervous system: ARNIB
    B R A I N
17. chemical messengers produced by the endocrine glands: SHORNMOE
    H O R M O N E S
18. part of question 16 where thinking takes place: CREUMBER
    C E R E B R U M
19. part of question 16 that helps you keep your balance: MULERBECLE
    C E R E B E L L U M
20. transfers electrical impulses from the eye to the brain: COPTI VERNE
    O P T I C   N E R V E
21. part of question 16 that connects to the spinal cord: DELUALM
    M E D U L L A
22. a quick, involuntary action: FELEXR
    R E F L E X
23. system that controls body functions such as sexual development: CODENINER
    E N D O C R I N E
24. the light-sensitive layer of cells at the back of the eye: ETNRAI
    R E T I N A
25. special neurons in the eye that detect light: EPSERROOPTHTCO
    P H O T O R E C E P T O R S
26. electrical messages that pass along the neurons: SPULIMES
    I M P U L S E S
27. type of question 25 that can detect very dim light: DSRO
    R O D S

Name ______________ Date ______ Class ______

CHAPTER 22 REINFORCEMENT WORKSHEET

Reproduction Review

Complete this worksheet after you finish reading Chapter 22, Section 1.

Different organisms reproduce in different ways. Fill in the table below by circling the correct type of reproduction. Then indicate the organism's method of fertilization and where the embryo develops. Several boxes have been filled in to get you started.

Organism	Type of reproduction	Method of fertilization	Where the embryo develops
Hydra	(asexual) or sexual	none	none (no embryo)
Whale	asexual or (sexual)	internal	inside the mother (placental)
Chicken	asexual or (sexual)	internal	in eggs outside the mother
Frog	asexual or (sexual)	internal or external	in eggs outside the mother
Sea star	(asexual) or sexual	none	none
Echidna	asexual or (sexual)	internal	in eggs outside the mother
Fish	asexual or (sexual)	internal or external	in eggs outside the mother
Human	asexual or (sexual)	internal	inside the mother (placental)
Kangaroo	asexual or (sexual)	internal	in a pouch outside the mother

Name ______________ Date ______ Class ______

CHAPTER 22 REINFORCEMENT WORKSHEET

The Beginning of a Life

Complete this worksheet after you have finished reading Chapter 22, Section 3.

The following illustration shows the development of a human. Choose the term from the list below left that best labels what is indicated in the diagram, and write the term in the corresponding box. Then, match each feature below right to the stage where it develops, and write the corresponding letter in the blank. Each feature and term is used once. Stages may have more than one feature.

Terms

umbilical cord
birth
fertilization
amnion
fetus
implantation
placenta
embryo

Developing features

A. hands and feet
B. hearing
C. formation of memories
D. beating heart tube
E. muscle movement
F. blinking and swallowing
G. taste buds and eyebrows
H. lungs "practice breathing"
I. limb buds and facial features
J. beginning of brain and spinal cord

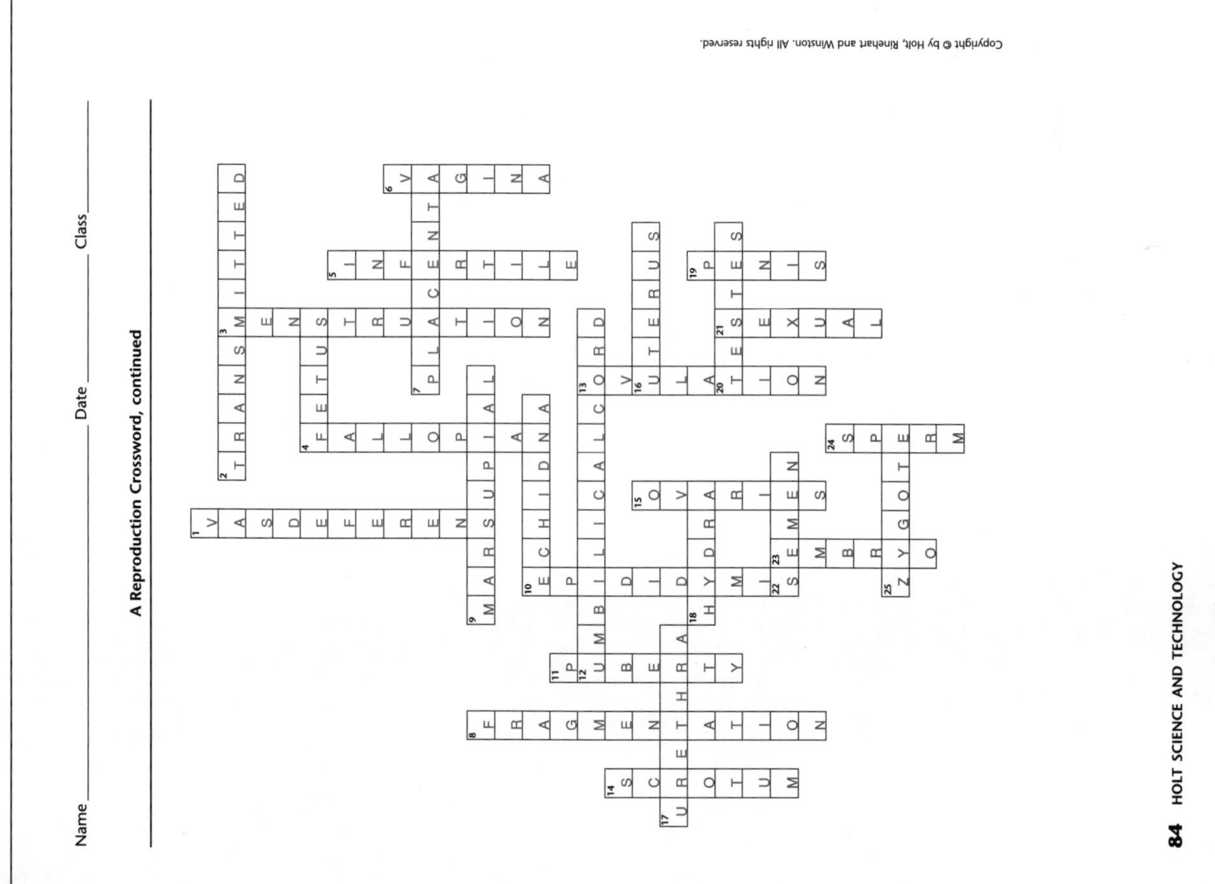
Name
Date
Class
A Reproduction Crossword, continued
84 HOLT SCIENCE AND TECHNOLOGY
Copyright © by Holt, Rinehart and Winston. All rights reserved.